unlearning church New Edition

Michael Slaughter

unlearning church New Edition

Foreword by Leonard Sweet

Abingdon Press
Nashville

UNLEARNING CHURCH
NEW EDITION
Copyright © 2002, 2008 by Michael Slaughter

This book is printed on acid-free paper.

Library of Congress Cataloging-in-Publication Data

Slaughter, Michael.
  Unlearning church / Michael Slaughter ; foreword by Leonard Sweet. -- New ed.
    p. cm.
  ISBN 978-0-687-64708-8 (pbk. : alk. paper)
  1. Christian leadership. I. Title.

  BV652.1.S585 2008
  253--dc22
                          2008021640

Scripture quotations, unless otherwise indicated, are from the New Revised Standard Version of the Bible, copyright 1989, Division of Christian Education of the National Council of the Churches of Christ in the United States of America. Used by permission. All rights reserved.

Scripture quotations noted The Message are from *THE MESSAGE*. Copyright © by Eugene H. Peterson 1993, 1994, 1995, 1996, 2000, 2001, 2002. Used by permission of NavPress Publishing Group.

Scripture quotations noted NIV are from the Holy Bible, NEW INTERNATIONAL VERSION®. Copyright © 1973, 1978, 1984 by International Bible Society. All rights reserved throughout the world. Used by permission of International Bible Society.

Scripture quotations noted KJV are from the King James or Authorized Version of the Bible.

08 09 10 11 12 13 14 15 16 17—10 9 8 7 6 5 4 3 2 1

MANUFACTURED IN THE UNITED STATES OF AMERICA

Contents

Foreword

We hear and apprehend only that which we already half-know.

—Henry David Thoreau

I came of age in a world that believed in "experts." I grew up in an academic world that actually believed scholarship and scientific knowledge could solve all the problems of the world: poverty, racism, crime, and so forth. Just do good enough research, get all the facts together, write a paper that uses the scientific method to formulate a solution, submit the formula to peer review, and . . .

Presto! Problem solved.

Adolf Hitler called this the "rule of experts" or "*Fuhrerprinzip*," which literally means the right of superior minds to command unquestioning obedience and special treatment.

Fuhrerprinzip is finished. What killed the "rule of experts"? First, the solutions that "experts" came up with often made the problems worse and/or created new problems.

Second, experts lied and lost trust. Two examples: In spite of reassurances from health experts and governmental sources, (a) eating contaminated beef really could cause "Mad Cow Disease" (BSE), and (b) the combined measles/mumps/rubella vaccine in Britain is now linked to a growing incidence of bowel disease and autism.

2

Third, scientific studies themselves demonstrate that the "common people," when given the right information and time to make conclusions, are "wiser" on social policy issues than social scientists and other "experts."

That's why I often begin my presentations with the disclaimer, "Don't take it from me."

In the modern world, "experts" asked us to "take it from me."

Forget it. Don't take it from me. I boast no immaculate perceptions. Like everyone else, I see "through a glass, dimly." I know only "in part." All perception is smudged. There is in my life a large element of not-knowing.

I know just enough to know that I don't know as much as I should know. The people to fear are those who don't know enough to know that they don't know. Willard Quine, who some claim was the most important philosopher of the second half of the twentieth century, took all the "?" keys off his typewriters. He quipped that he didn't need them because he dealt in certainties.

Really, Mr. Quine!

I am like the seminary professor with the "80/20 rule": He claimed that 80 percent of his theology was right and 20 percent was wrong. He just didn't know which was which. I don't even agree with myself and some of the things I wrote ten years ago. Don't believe what I say because you believe me. You must know inside yourself that what I'm saying is true. All I'm doing is giving you a template for your use in testing your own experiences and observations.

One person paid me the ultimate compliment: "Dr. Sweet, this is the fourth time I've heard you. You certainly are interesting. But I'm going to tell you something. You never tell me anything I don't already know, but until you say it, I don't know I know it."

Don't take it from me.

If what I'm saying doesn't ring true in your soul or ring a bell in your brain, I could be wrong. That could be my 20 percent. Of course, that could also be your 20 percent. Either way, we need to check each other and test the Spirit.

Don't take it from Mike Slaughter either.

If you don't already know inside that what Mike is saying is true . . .

If, as you're reading what follows, you aren't saying, "Hey, I already knew that—I just didn't have the words for it . . ."

If Mike is not saying things here that you've already felt deep inside but not brought to consciousness . . .

If this book doesn't illuminate what you think but didn't know you thought until you read it here . . .

Then don't take it from Mike.

But if, as you read this book, you find yourself saying over and over again, as I did, "Oh, I see . . . I see . . ."

If God is giving us flashes of insight: "Aha . . . Amen . . ."

If God is opening in us an awareness of "that's right . . . of course . . ."

Then we're not taking it from Mike.

We're taking it from the Spirit.

The Holy Spirit is resonating with both our spirits and Mike's spirit to move us from belief to faith, from "ought" and "should" to "must." Besides, as Mike is the first to tell us, it's not about him anyway. It's all about Jesus and his "must" claims in our lives.

UnLearning Church is a "must" book for church leaders.

Leonard Sweet
E. Stanley Jones Professor of Evangelism
Drew Theological School
Madison, New Jersey
www.LeonardSweet.com

Introduction

A friend who is under thirty-five told me this story of a major transition that happened in his life and ministry:

When God began to nudge my wife and me toward starting a church, I began looking for someone who was "doing church right." I had grown up in churches that pushed me to participate in worship and ministry but in which very few people actually met Jesus and became a part of those communities.

My search led me to attend a conference at a well-known teaching church. I was so inspired about reaching lost people that I remember crying with joy intermittently through many of the talks. My wife and I set out to plant a church just like the one I had visited. At conference time the next year, I brought all our key people from the new congregation we were launching in Clemson, South Carolina. We each left the conference ready to build that church in our state.

It took us about six months to realize that something was seriously wrong.

It wasn't working, our generation wasn't responding, and I felt like quitting. It was as if we were putting on a big performance that left people unaffected.

Fortunately, God is faithful and taught us in our discouragement. He used the teaching church to free me to be creative and think outside the box and inside the Spirit's leading. God took that freedom and many of the things I had been taught growing up about a more participative church and blended them into something that appealed to and changed Clemson students. We made a bunch of changes all at once, and lives began to turn toward Jesus. We moved from a school auditorium to a bar, from morning gatherings to night gatherings, and from lousy music to a solid worship band.

More important, what really changed us and the course of the church was our move to make high-engagement worship central to everything we did. We became worshipers and a real family. We began to build a faith community that experienced worship, a sense of family, and personal growth. The church expanded rapidly toward God and numerically over the next three years.

—*John Reeves*

UnLearning Church is about people like John. I hope it is also about people like you.

The following pages address the unique qualities of *your* church, *your* community, *your* leadership, and *your* life. This book is about leaders in churches, old and young, daring to leave the status quo and fearlessly stepping out into God's promising and yet unknown future. It's about "unLearners" on the cutting edge of how God works best—through unique personalities localized to their context. It's about the prophetic witness to Christ's presence in individual communities with a ripple effect reaching around the world.

No longer can any one community of Christ's followers dictate what another church must do to succeed. I'm "unLearning" the model of cloning someone else's blueprint. That era is over. God's kingdom is not best represented by franchises of McChurch. If you focus your energies on copying someone else's methodologies or programs, you will miss something crucially important.

The Holy Spirit is empowering transformational leaders who demonstrate the kingdom of God in unique ways in each different community. That's a world of difference from copying someone else's ministry and building a "been there, done that, bought the T-shirt" look-alike.

Every church leader has a specific call and distinguishing gift base of talent. You already have the God-given gifts you need. Your mission is to use them to excel in a local implementation of the overall mission of Jesus Christ. Your effectiveness in the future will be measured by how well your church demonstrated the kingdom of God in unique ways to your indigenous community and beyond. Your goal is to connect people to an authentic experience of God in this world.

An Ancient-Future Answer

Today's emerging churches are anchoring themselves in the ancient truths of biblical authority, yet they're operating in an atmosphere of innovation and change. Armed with a strong sense of "first causes," they're forming distinctive communities of faith. They are safe spaces for spiritually hungry hearts, environments of deep connection, experiences of community, and centers of involvement in the pursuit of social justice.

The surrounding culture has significantly changed in recent years. This book is an urgent call for spiritual and prophetic leadership toward the new developments in our culture. The question is not "What is Ginghamsburg (or *Pick-Your-Favorite* Church) doing these days?" Nor is the motivation to climb the American ladder named bigger-better-more.

The call is to unLearn—to break the rules of conventional wisdom in order to translate God's ancient purposes to today's postmodern world. The challenge is to translate and target those purposes to each indigenous environment. This book is about visualizing and articulating alternative pathways of ministry based on who you are and how God has uniquely gifted you. It addresses the fulfillment of your life mission as a church leader, your specific commitment to spiritual growth, and your ministry focus for the next year.

This book is organized into two parts:

Part 1 shows how unLearning CHURCHES connect people with a high-touch experience of God in a high-tech world. These chapters will help you formulate a vision of what God wants to do through your church.

Part 2 shows how unLearning LEADERSHIP empowers servants of God to do the mission of Jesus. These chapters will guide you in making God's vision a reality in your own unique context, with the group of people God has called together for this purpose.

You can create environments in which people can become radical followers of Jesus Christ. As God asked the prophet Jeremiah, to whom he'd given great vision, "What do you see?" each chapter challenges you to describe the vision God is creating in you.

What old habits and worldviews must you unLearn in order to make that vision a reality? What does the next step look like?

Radical Abandonment and Evangelism

UnLearning is not about continuing what you are already doing and simply slapping on a new slogan, better technology, or some other additive. The goal of this book is not to showcase the latest program or to give you a numbered list of how-to steps. The challenge in these pages is to hear and obey God with a sense of radical abandonment. The result will be new ways of ministering to people, using the resources God has already given to you.

Radical abandonment to Jesus is much more holistic than a set of prescriptive formulas. Jesus rose from the grave, looked at his disciples, and said, "You will receive power" (Acts 1:8). A revolutionary power. An uncommon power. Power to be witnesses in the power of the Holy Spirit.

The challenge is to find and follow God's directive *for you*. Your local implementation may take on a one-of-a-kind flavor seen nowhere else. Yet the results will be similar: You'll design communities invaded by the presence of God through Jesus Christ that demonstrate the very kingdom of God. Radical Christianity is being the hands and feet of Jesus Christ, led and empowered by the Holy Spirit, ready to serve and give witness whenever and to whomever God calls us to reach, in ways uniquely appropriate for each particular community. Consider these two examples:

Everything about Princeton Alliance Church at the Crossroads says, "Urban professionals are welcome here." The church campus in New Jersey's research corridor was intentionally constructed to look like the executive office parks nearby. Each church ministry models a quality standard consistent with the surrounding business community. Not surprisingly, the church has made great inroads for Christ with executives and managers at nearby Merrill Lynch, Bloomberg, and Bristol-Myers Squibb. "Our calling is to reach everyone we can," says pastor Bob Cushman, "but we know we're best at connecting with urban professionals, so that's why we build a corporate feel into all we do."

Six hundred miles to the southwest, Quest Community Church in Lexington, Kentucky, has a similar passion for outreach but does best at impacting a different community. Pastor Pete Hise is proud of the fact that 25 percent of the people who attend Sunday mornings are either atheists or agnostics. He's particularly glad that young people with body piercings find lots of others at the church who look like them. "Which church in Lexington will reach that kind of person for Jesus?" he asks. "The one gaping hole in most churches' ministry is in reaching the Generation X crowd. That's what we do best." He estimates that as many as three hundred thousand people in greater Lexington need to hear about Jesus in a way they have not yet heard.

These two churches share the same overall mission of turning irreligious people into committed followers of Christ, but the local expressions are completely different. Each is appropriate for some segment of its community. Each of these churches has found its own flavor.

It's time to go beyond knowing and believing God's truth to experiencing and demonstrating God's presence. God wants you to be authentic, the real deal, becoming a change agent for the entire world.

Start by UnLearning

To become an indigenous, relevant community, you will unLearn lots of things you thought were right.

UnLearning is about going a different direction. UnLearning means repentance. It requires us to identify ways we were wrong and to rebuild in a new direction. UnLearning is about breaking away from the pack, because a crowd will always be slower to respond to the radical voice of Jesus Christ. UnLearning is about ways the Holy Spirit can adjust your leadership skills and attitudes. Then you, in turn, can lead the way for a similar transformation in others. Most important, unLearning is about experience.

Leaders who unLearn are a different breed from what you may be used to. They are willing to fail. They break their own rules—at least the rules that prohibit people from becoming passionate followers of Jesus. UnLearning churches demonstrate an uncompromising approach to church mission and ministry. The methods may seem new, but the approach follows an ancient call.

Why a book about unLearning? Any navigator who travels fluid waters knows the need to change the angle of a boat's sails as soon as the wind blows from a new direction. Today's ocean of constantly changing pop-culture breezes may make you uncomfortable. That's a good thing. Discomfort precedes change. Tension spurs learning and growth. It's important for you to ask questions that other leaders may not be asking. Now is the time to seriously evaluate what you're doing in light of the fresh wind of God's Spirit blowing through a post-Christian world.

UnLearning Church will inspire you to create a safe space, an environment in which people are free to become radical followers of Jesus Christ. This book will challenge how you see and do church. It will speak to both head and heart, and chances are you'll find yourself on an unexpected spiritual journey.

Are you ready to take yourself and your church on that kind of journey? Ready to unLearn anything in your church, leadership, or lifestyle that stands in the way? God is calling people to develop faith communities that effectively reach unchurched populations for Jesus Christ in a postmodern, post-Christian world—radical disciples abandoned to the purpose of evangelism through relevant service.

Want to be there? Then let's begin unLearning.

unLearning Church

CASTING THE VISION

1 Born to Be Wild

UnLearning churches defy old identities. They don't fit into the usual categories. They're tough to label, difficult to classify, and downright unpredictable. UnLearning churches are based on shared life in Jesus—not issue-centered ideology. The people at the helm are fully dependent on the leading of the unseen Spirit of God.

"Church growth" was the mantra of the 1980s and 1990s. I attended my first "Breaking the Two Hundred Barrier" conference shortly after becoming Ginghamsburg's pastor in 1979. Then I enrolled in "Breaking Four Hundred" and "Breaking Eight Hundred."

We became experts at methodologies that involved small group and Sunday school ministries. When it was trendy to do so, we shifted from a programmatic approach to a cell-driven approach. We began to develop associations around the successful megachurches of that day. We learned about the pastor as CEO, and I adopted that model. In the late 1990s, I really thought the contemporary megachurch would be the church of the future. It was the kind of church almost everyone seemed to aspire to become. Our culture preferred Wal-Mart superstores to the corner drugstore and giant Home Depots to local hardware stores. It made sense for churches to follow that same pattern.

To move forward, I have had to unLearn the megachurch and CEO models. If we continue to copy the models of the 1980s and 1990s, we're going to miss the next generation. I'm now learning to take my cues from the age-group that's under thirty-five. A one-size-fits-all approach toward growth will definitely not be the most effective model of the twenty-first century.

Change is so constant today that no one can predict the effective church of the future, yet I don't believe it will be the shopping-mall-size megachurch. As many growing churches have demonstrated, once you exceed an attendance of four hundred, a majority of growth can be transfer growth from already-churched populations. Some megachurches have seen success in reaching unchurched populations, but too often church growth in the United States and Canada does not represent net gains for the kingdom of God.

A seismic shift is occurring in the practice of church. Emerging churches are defying many of the formulas of the late-twentieth-century church-growth movement. The newest islands of health and hope are not the "Fortune 500 churches"—the established models of the 1980s and 1990s that everyone was trying to clone. A new breed of churches is emerging, led by a new generation of young innovators who noticeably resist trying to duplicate the successful church-growth models of the last century.

What's Your "One Thing"?

Like those two churches I described above, unLearning churches are finding their special niche where they can connect with certain people better than any other church can. I recently visited five growing churches in Oklahoma City, each with one thousand or more in attendance, but they're all distinct in the ways they are appealing to and serving that city. They are not all trying to look like the same megachurch model. One church emphasizes the Creation. Its campus is full of waterfalls and living plants, and it sponsors a wide diversity of life-generating ministries in the community, from an eye clinic in the inner city to programs for ex-offenders. Another communicates the atmosphere of a high-class hotel, featuring a more classical appearance and reaching the upper-middle class with strong ministries to singles and blended families.

These churches may all share the same geographic area, but they are reaching distinctly different people groups. The distinctiveness of churches like these goes far beyond denominational differences and worship styles. They don't fit the same old classifications and they can't be traced to the same cookie-cutter mold. They all take a different tack, but they all excel in local implementation. They connect people in their communities or cultures to an experience of God, to authentic community, and to life purpose.

If the emerging church is recognized and valued for anything, it's for a highly effective, indigenous carrying out of the mission of Jesus Christ. This next generation of churches goes far beyond a simple name change from "Methodist" or "Baptist" to "Community Church" or "Christian Center." These churches resist such categories as traditional or contemporary; conservative or liberal; large or small; suburban, urban, or rural; and even Catholic or Protestant. They don't fit neatly into categorized boxes. Each of their hearts is to uniquely demonstrate the presence of God in their own native settings.

UnLearning churches each articulate and practice a unique call and identity. Like the four friends who brought the paralyzed man to Jesus by cutting a hole in the roof (Mark 2:3-4), these prophetic communities find creative ways to bring people to Jesus. The dominant expression of Christianity at Ginghamsburg is service. People primarily express their faith in Jesus by serving in a multitude of ways. For other churches, that unique call might be a healing ministry or the sending out of daughter churches.

The specific mission and style of your congregation won't necessarily be the same as mine or anybody else's. Try to put a finger on God's vision for your church as you experience this book. I also encourage you to make specific commitments to spiritual growth that may help you get in touch with that unique vision.

Patron Saints of Unlearning

For any organization to have an impact, it needs a radical product. The church's radical product is revolutionary people—real followers of Jesus Christ, whom I describe in a previous book, *Real Followers: Beyond Virtual Christianity* (Abingdon, 1999). As churches take seriously Jesus' call to discipleship, their memberships change from consumer mind-sets to missional movements of God whose members demonstrate both personal and social holiness.

When I used to hear the word *church*, I thought of something innocuous, boring, and bland. Christianity was nothing more than "nice-ianity." But once I started reading the New Testament, I discovered that Christianity is anything but nice. It is extreme. Everywhere these people went, scandal, fear, and violence followed them. Theirs was a radical faith!

Think about the Christmas story, especially the unprecedented, supernatural way Mary became pregnant. If you were Joseph, shocked to hear that your fiancée, Mary, had a baby in her womb, would you believe the dream in which an angel of the Lord appeared to you? The angel said, "Joseph, son of David, do not be afraid to take Mary as your wife, for the child conceived in her is from the Holy Spirit" (Matthew 1:20).

Everything within Joseph told him that the best thing to do would be to divorce Mary quietly. Instead, he acted on an intuitive sense of the Spirit. He took a huge risk in how he followed God.

Fast-forward thirty years or so. The disciples, riding in a small boat on the Sea of Galilee and battling fierce waves and winds, saw Jesus walking calmly across the water. They were all terrified. Most of them couldn't recognize him, and thought it must be a ghost. Only Peter got out of the boat and walked on water because his faith told him that it was Jesus out there.

Peter was the only one who risked. He chose to block out the voice of the storm. Instead, he focused on Jesus, who said, "Come." Peter did the impossible because he responded to the voice of Jesus instead of listening to the crashing waves and the fearful cries of others. He only got in trouble when he began to look at the raging storm rather than look into the eyes of the one who had said, "Follow me" (Matthew 4:19). Still, Peter was not a failure because he looked down and began to sink. If anyone failed, it was the eleven who stayed in the boat, waiting to see if it could be done.

That same risk-taking shows up in dynamic people throughout history. Imagine, for example, growing up in eighteenth-century Europe, when slavery was a long-established, virtually unchallenged tradition. Everyone around you said that slavery was normal, natural, unavoidable, and perhaps even necessary. Yet a Christian named William Wilberforce saw the unseen and took a faith risk. In 1789 he led a campaign against the British slave trade. He continued to champion the impossible. In 1807 the impossible happened: Great Britain abolished the slave trade in the British colonies. In 1833 an act of Parliament called for the emancipation of slaves throughout the British Empire.

Here in the United States, a man named Millard Fuller believed he could change the face of housing for the poor in America. He founded an organization called Habitat for Humanity, which has built more than one hundred thousand homes around the world for people in need—all "because of Jesus," he says. "We are putting God's love into action."[1]

Even our fantasy world applauds the idea of taking risks to do the impossible. In the movie *Indiana Jones and the Last Crusade*, Indiana steps out onto a bridge that isn't yet there, or at least doesn't seem to be there. Instead of falling to his death, however, he rests his foot on something solid but heretofore unseen.

God has chosen you, called you, gifted you, and promised a fulfillment of your life mission. God would not create you for failure. Your success is based on your willingness to risk stepping out and obediently following God. All of us experience seasons of doubt and frustration; unLearning leaders step out of the boat anyway.

Frighteningly and Radically Called

I remember one of my first encounters with God. It seemed God was chasing me. It was the summer of 1967, and I was at a real low point in my life. Two of my friends had just been busted for drugs. My mom and dad were frustrated with me. They decided to send me down south to visit relatives I had never met. They wanted to "keep me in touch with my roots," they said.

During that time, I would lie, cheat, or do anything to get what I wanted. I even had some help at breaking the rules. A few days before graduation from high school, one teacher changed an F to a D so I could graduate. In another class, I copied off of someone else's exam so I could pass. I had no interest in doing what pleased God.

Yet God was chasing me, and these God-whispers would pop up everywhere I went. In fact, all these God-whispers troubled me so much that I remember calling my girlfriend long-distance to talk about it. God had never bothered me like this before. God even went ahead of me into the restroom of a two-pump gas station in the backwaters of rural Arkansas. There, scrawled on the wall above the urinal, were these words: "Jesus saves all who want him."

The outcome of this experience and others in the ensuing months was life changing. I truly encountered the resurrected Jesus Christ, which ultimately changed everything. Jesus saved me, and I wanted him. My encounter with God in my late teens was revolutionary. From that time forward, I knew I wanted to reach a target population that has been turned off or out by the established church. This group represents a huge number of people. On any given weekend, up to three-quarters of Americans[2]—and an even higher number of Canadians[3]—are not in church. Those are the people I want to reach. I'm thankful for congregations that nurture the already churched, but I'm interested in finding ways to speak to the unchurched.

Jesus moved into my life, changing my priorities, my values, and my relationships. He transformed everything in my life. "Christ in me" is the source of resurrection power. It comes only through my being dead, buried, and out of the way. When we say "yes" to Jesus, we are "buried with him by baptism into death, so that, just as Christ was raised from the dead by the glory of the Father, so we too might walk in newness of life" (Romans 6:4).

I want to invest my life in those who want to pursue radical Christianity. The emerging leader is not enamored with the latest religion of self-actualization. The religion of talk-show television is a rudderless spirituality. Jesus calls us to self-expenditure, not self-infatuation. He says, "If any want to become my followers, let them deny themselves and take up their cross daily and follow me. For those who want to save their life will lose it, and those who lose their life for my sake will save it" (Luke 9:23-24).

I don't want to lead a megachurch of people who come together to be inspired to live status-quo lives peppered with Judeo-Christian values. I want to empower radical followers of Jesus.

Transformation, Not Information

People today, both inside and outside the church, have an apathetic attitude toward organized religion. Most will tell you that it's not working. Perhaps their lack of interest is because we institutional church people have been more skilled at building walls of dogma and exclusivity than at rediscovering ancient paths of life-transformation.

Our society is marked by increased spiritual hunger and activity, yet overall attendance in churches has decreased. The number of people in attendance weekly in United Methodist churches has been declining for years—dramatically so. The same is true in most other mainline denominations. This decline seems to accompany a lack of spiritual power in churches today. As I look around many churches, the situation seems like the movie *Night of the Living Dead*. Many churches have died, and someone just needs to tell them they're dead. The churches that are still alive are asking, like the prophet Elijah, "Am I the only one left? Is there anyone out there who is being faithful to the purpose of God on planet Earth?" (See 1 Kings 19:1-10.)

Remember the guy who burst into a Baptist church in Texas? If angry people with guns are going to storm into church gatherings and shoot folks for their faith relationship with Jesus Christ, then I want to get shot for being a part of the right thing. I don't want the church I serve to sacrifice lives to something that is not world-changing.

For the earliest Christians, the gospel wasn't about information, but about a revolutionary encounter with God—"what we have heard . . . seen with our eyes . . . and touched with our hands . . . the eternal life that was with the Father and was revealed to us" (1 John 1:1b-2). After his resurrection, Jesus warned his followers not to go out alone, but to "wait there for the promise of the Father" when they would be "baptized with the Holy Spirit" (Acts 1:4-5). Think about the implications of that order. Jesus' followers had been with him for three years. (That's a whole lot better than attending a weeklong church growth conference.) Didn't they learn enough about Jesus by watching and copying his work? Apparently not. Jesus was telling his followers, in effect, that information and imitation were not enough.

As a child in Sunday school, I received information about the man named Jesus. My teacher gave me a little picture of Jesus to carry around in my wallet. It was about the size of a baseball card. You've probably seen this picture, found in many Protestant church buildings in the 1950s and 1960s—the wavy hair, the aura of light around his head. I came to think about Jesus as a player featured on the baseball cards I collected. (Unfortunately, this little picture wasn't worth as much as a baseball card!) I often wonder what would have happened if I had said to my baseball-card-collecting buddies, "I have a '58 Jesus in mint condition; what will you give me for it?" It seemed that faith was measured by the ability to quote facts and memorize trivia about a historical player. It was just like memorizing the statistics about a baseball legend, based on information on the back of the card.

UnLearning Moment

What do you need to unLearn in order to make your church a place of transformation and not just information?

You probably remember the WWJD fad of the late 1990s and early 2000s. People wore bracelets and displayed bumper stickers all designed to help us ask ourselves, "What would Jesus do?" The idea is to try to determine what Jesus would do in a situation and then to imitate Jesus' response. But knowledge and imitation of Jesus' behavior and are not enough. First John 4:9 says, "God's love was revealed among us in this way: God sent his only Son into the world so that we might live through him." The purpose is that we might *live* through him, not that we might merely *believe* in him. Living for God is not about imitation or information—it requires transformation. The Spirit of God must live in us.

Vessels of the Spirit

In Old Testament times, fire often signified God's presence. When Moses led the Israelites through the desert, God was as close as a cloud during the day and a pillar of fire during the night. When the people saw the fire, they remembered God's promise of daily provision, protection, and power for living. When God moved, they moved. When God stopped, they stopped, even for months at a time. The idea was to place themselves at the heart of God's leadership and direction.

At the time the fire of God's Holy Spirit was limited to one place, usually above the tent where they met for worship. The Spirit would sometimes come upon Moses, and sometimes others. When Jesus was on planet Earth, the Holy Spirit in him was limited to one physical body. Jesus could be in only one place at a time; but when Jesus ascended to heaven and sent the Holy Spirit to earth in a new way, everything changed. Since Pentecost, the Holy Spirit has been made available to all people. No longer is God merely with us, now God is in us. Jesus can be everywhere we are, all around the world at the same time. We are literally the body of Christ on earth, where people come and experience love, acceptance, forgiveness, freedom from fear, release from guilt and discouragement, delivery from loneliness, and empowerment for living.

At age seventeen I couldn't see the future. All I could focus on was the draft for the Vietnam War. This was about a year after my God-encounter at that gas station in rural Arkansas, but I was still filled with fear and anxiety, rather than with the Holy Spirit. I used to go across the street and play pool with a guy in my neighborhood who was in his fifties and who had studied for the priesthood. There was something different—a peace—about this guy. He knew Jesus in a way I didn't. I'd talk about my fears, and he'd talk about Jesus.

Sometimes you have a better chance of seeing Jesus while shooting pool than you do in the church. I said to this would-be priest, "I am going to be eighteen on my next birthday. I can't see past eighteen, and it really scares me. I think this may be some kind of premonition that I am going to die or something."

My comments opened the door for several conversations about my friend's experience with Jesus. I can't explain what happened because it wasn't like a crisis moment, but somehow during those "close encounters," I began to experience the mystery of the powerful Jesus. My eyes were opened, and I could see the future. Eternal life divinely invaded my body and the Spirit began to live in me. It was strange. My heart began to beat in rhythm with God's heart. My eyes began to see through God's eyes. My mind began to think with God's mind.

I was seventeen, but suddenly I could see my future! I could see how my life was going to be used for God's purpose to touch other people. I could see God's future and plan. It wasn't like I fully understood it, but I trusted the one who did, and tried to follow even when God's plan didn't coincide with my own. During my first two years in college, I studied retail management. I was going to make some serious money. The next thing I knew, I found myself in the School of Social Work, working with Appalachian folks. What happened? Jesus transformed me.

Many people come to Jesus and then expect Jesus to become converted to *their* worldview. But God is not the one who needs to change. To experience Jesus is to take on Jesus' worldview, to allow ourselves to be radically transformed. We must take on Jesus' outlook, Jesus' perspective, and Jesus' priorities. If we're going to be the church at all, let's be the real thing.

The opening words of 1 John refer to Jesus as the word of life, the Word of God. A lot of people believe that God "spoke" (past tense) only through scripture. True, Scripture is the word of God, but God is still speaking (present tense) through Jesus. The prophets in the Bible never limited God to "God said long ago." They used the phrase "thus saith the Lord." They remind us that God is continually speaking. The living Word of God is in you and me, speaking right now. Jesus continues to speak and to transform you and me. That is the mystery of the powerful Jesus. The world is looking for a radical experience of God.

UnLearning churches will follow God's leading, much as God's people of old did in following the pillar of fire. The body of Christ has a rudder that goes deep into the ways of God as revealed in scripture. Our religion is ancient in that it is "the faith that was once for all entrusted to the saints" (Jude 3b). It is future in that it's being played out in a spiritual atmosphere of innovation and change. The people of God are directed to be continually about the new thing that God is doing. "See, I am doing a new thing," God says in Isaiah 43. "Do you not perceive it?" (43:19 NIV). The unLearning church will keep its eye on the Holy Spirit, watching where God is moving, where God is taking the church next. As Jesus said, "The wind blows where it chooses. . . . So it is with everyone who is born of the Spirit" (John 3:8). When we follow the Spirit with reckless abandon, we become willing to innovate, re-create, reassess, step out, and risk going wherever God is moving.

One Church That's UnLearning

Mosaic, Los Angeles, California
www.mosaic.org

- **Quick Description:** A community that lives by faith, is known by love, and offers a voice of hope.
- **History:** Southern Baptist; started in Los Angeles in1953, and now has locations in downtown Los Angeles, Beverly Hills, Pasadena, the Inland Empire, Berkeley, and Whittier, with two more campuses in Hollywood and the South Bay in formation.

- **Attendance:** 3,000 at eight worship celebrations across the Los Angeles and San Francisco areas.

"I'm unLearning the way Jesus touches people through people. We give the small things to Jesus, while bringing our bigger issues to Freud. We've lost confidence in Jesus' ability to heal, transform, and make us whole. Jesus is interested in making whole disciples out of broken people. God specializes in fixing broken relationships. We were created for the purpose of intimate companionship with him. We lack power and credibility if we offer to others a level of relationship we don't know in reality ourselves. We at Mosaic don't focus on growing the church but on connecting people with the kingdom of God through Jesus. We are not about church growth; we're about doing the right things. That attitude costs us a lot of growth. Our front door is the transformed lives of our people. If you get people in the right environments, where Jesus shows up, their lives will change forever."

—Erwin McManus, lead pastor, has been a part of
Mosaic since 1992; age: late forties

From Broadcast to Narrowcast

Our culture today is all about personalization. UnLearning churches focus on personalized pathways of discipleship that meet individual needs, rather than one-size-fits-all programs for the masses. They shift the emphasis from quantity to quality and from church growth to church health.

On the social networking website Facebook, there are groups for young adults who love Abraham Lincoln trivia, Mississippians advocating better posture, math majors looking for dates, and people who spell their last name Conner rather than Connor. If you happen to spell your last name Konner, you can start a group for that too, with just a few clicks of the mouse.

Amazon.com will remember if you browsed baseball books last week and recommends *Rob Neyer's Big Book of Baseball Blunders* the next time you log on. The Weather Channel's website will recall your zip code and tell you it's going to rain tomorrow without your having to reenter your city and state. Rather than just any old website of stock tips, you can customize the home pages to become "My Fidelity," "My AOL Personal Finance," or "My CitiCorp." You can order Levi's jeans to your exact measurements, and specify what mix of programs and features you want on your new Dell laptop. Advertisements promise that the product or service they promote will perfectly suit your needs and wants. As one of Microsoft's advertising campaigns asked, "Where do *you* want to go today?"

Our culture has gone from broadcast to narrowcast, recognizing and capitalizing on the likes and dislikes, quirks and concerns of every potential consumer. Business and marketing today model the art of speaking to the individual. It's what Faith Popcorn referred to as the economy of "ego-nomics"[1]—everything is focused on what you want, when you want it, where you want it. Savvy businesses understand that they can no longer focus on the masses. They have unLearned the starting point of attracting crowds and replaced it with meeting individuals at the point of their felt needs in the now. In the age of the Internet, you have to think smaller to grow bigger.

Emerging churches will unLearn the assumptions that bigger is always better and that a wider net always catches more fish. UnLearning churches are offering smaller worship venues and more specific Bible study topics, so that people can gather in more intimate settings with people who share their interests and needs. If we are to reach future generations, we must offer a personalized pathway of discipleship that is designed to meet people's individual needs.

From Broadcast to Podcast

Consider, for example, the way preachers reach their audiences now as compared to centuries past. During the age of modernity, the great revivals were based on broadcast. The idea was to assemble large groups of people in large public venues to hear a great presenter, from Jonathan Edwards, Charles Finney, and Dwight Moody to Luis Palau, T. D. Jakes, and Billy Graham. Radio and television brought great preaching into private homes, but such broadcasts were still limited by the scheduling restraints of the channel they aired on. In the postmodern era, sermons are posted online as downloadable podcasts that reach people one at a time, right where they are, at home with their laptop or jogging with their iPod.

Our www.ginghamsburg.org site supports more than two dozen different online fellowship communities. Some are broad-based classifications. For example, several hundred people from around the globe converse weekly about the use of media and technology in the local church. They help one another sort out the details of media ministry. Others are highly focused, like new members and hospitality ministries, and have attracted a smaller, more intimate group of regular contributors. You can meet real people globally in highly personalized ways, all in the cyber-now, whatever your interest and style.

Within two years of launching our Ginghamsburg website, the number of weekly users matched the number of people on premises each weekend. By the third year, it exceeded our campus attendance by more than ten times! Here I live in an obscure town in Ohio, and we receive more than fifty thousand visits representing forty different countries to our site each month (as of late 2007). People around the world can see, hear, or read the weekend message by Sunday evening. I once received an e-mail from a young Japanese student, a Buddhist, writing from his dorm room in Japan. He was asking about something I had said about Jesus in my sermon. His culture sees spirituality in a very quiet, personal way; the Internet gives him the opportunity to explore it in the context of a safe space. By focusing on the individual, churches can reach countless people for Christ.

UnLearning from Those under Thirty-five

Today's church is too often still setting its agenda by the demographics of the baby boomers—those born from 1946 to 1964. In my experience, the successful growth churches of the 1980s and 1990s are usually made up of people in their forties and older. These people are primarily a modern-era audience, from which many of us in the church are still taking our cues when we attempt to address people's spiritual needs with simplistic answers and formulaic worship. Many attempts at renewal are still repeating what they did in the 1980s and 1990s when many baby boomers were reconnecting with church. Baby boomers were attracted to food courts in mega-malls, so churches tried to replicate those kinds of amenities. Millennials, on the other hand, are hanging out in Starbucks and wine bars, drawn by the casual, communal atmosphere that culturally savvy churches are now also offering. Jesus Christ is the same yesterday, today, and tomorrow, but the cultural language is continually changing. The formulas of the 1980s and 1990s won't work for the future with the millennial generations.

Postmodern-minded people view the cosmos as too complex to be defined and explained by the scientific method. They demonstrate an intense spiritual hunger left by the vacuum of modernity. They are open to a cafeteria-style spirituality, drawing wisdom and practices from a variety of religious traditions. Most are looking outside the Christian faith to find a sense of spiritual connection. Postmoderns are seeking an experience of the "Mysterious Other" but believe the religion of the church to be restricting.

UnLearning Moment

What boomer-era practice could you unLearn in order to better reach younger generations?

Moderns and postmoderns will continue alongside each other for some time. But to continue to take our cues from boomers will cause us to miss the next generations. To understand the seismic shift in today's changing worldview, we have to focus on the under-thirty-five age-group. More than anyone alive today, they tend to connect with what postmodernity is all about.

A few years ago, I began to examine emerging churches that are relating to the next demographic group. The focus in these churches has shifted away from the effective twentieth-century models that attracted large crowds to "hear" the gospel message.

These emerging churches are communities of personalization. They focus on meeting the real needs of people, offering Christ's life-transforming power exactly where and how people need to experience it.

Their most durable impact in shaping the future will be in this message to us boomers: If you think the goal is merely to build large churches with great music, incredible dramas, and media presentations, you may forget the real business you're in— radical life transformation through the power of God. It's all about spirit, not size!

Quality over Quantity

By today's standards, Jesus' three-year experience with his disciples would be considered a failure. He spent most of his energy on just twelve people, one of whom ended up failing miserably. At the end of Jesus' earthly ministry, his church had only 120 people, and his leadership ended in scandal as he was convicted and executed by religious authorities.

No one today would pay to go to Jesus' church-growth seminar. Yet you and I are Christ-followers today because of those 120 people and the worldwide movement they ignited. Instead of focusing on numbers of people, Jesus focused on the people themselves. Likewise, unLearning churches will focus more on church health than church growth. Healthy organisms grow naturally. Churches that are healthy tend to grow in size, but life transformation, not church growth, is their measure of success.

Being in Christ is about a life of quality, not quantity. Jesus did not say, "I came that you may have more stuff," or "I came that you may be elevated to higher positions." Jesus said, "I came that they [those who belong to him] may have life, and have it abundantly" (John 10:10b).

You and I yearn for meaning. We want our lives to count. God has woven into our beings a desire to pursue significance. We are wired for it. Yet even followers of Jesus can become so quickly distracted that we trade significance for temporal success. Jesus said greatness is who God is making you to be, not how much you have. Jesus' disciples had to unLearn their definition of greatness.

One day Jesus' close followers, Peter, James, and John, began arguing over which of them would be most important. They had just returned from a mountaintop retreat with Jesus. They had experienced the power of God and now, just a day later, were already being overcome with an exaggerated sense of their own importance. They were confusing self-centered success with God-centered purpose.

The Message phrases Jesus' response so well: "You become great by accepting, not asserting," Jesus said. Not grabbing, not controlling, not manipulating. "Your spirit, not your size, makes the difference," he concluded (Luke 9:48b).

In their atmospheres of innovation and change, unLearning churches focus on quality of experience rather than quantity of people. Success is not measured in numbers alone; it's about transformed lives.

Thousands of churches in the 1980s and 1990s focused on a barrier-breaking model. Popular conferences offered the management techniques needed to work with larger groups of people. Smaller churches tried to break the two-hundred barrier, and larger churches learned how to grow through the thousand barrier. Too many churches used those calibrations to concentrate more on quantity than quality. Too many of us measured our success by the number of people attending our worship services.

The unLearning church doesn't fixate on how it can grow toward human standards of greatness. It's preoccupied instead with how to be in the life-transforming mission business. Its leaders would jump at a chance to take on a community of one hundred radical followers of Jesus rather than a minimum-commitment crowd of several thousand.

At Ginghamsburg we've learned that sometimes our shifts to higher quality have cost us quantity. At one point, we phased out one of our Saturday night services so we could offer a talkback time after the 5:25 worship celebration. For those in attendance, this met a real need for personal interaction and changed lives. This strategic focus created some time constraints. It prevented us from leading a second celebration later that evening. We did what promoted life change, not what made the most business sense to gather the largest crowds. We committed ourselves to the real business of Jesus—life transformation—and not to the sometimes superficial business of church growth.

Narrowcasting in Action

Marketing professionals know the importance of identifying a potential consumer's "felt need," and tailoring their promotions to those needs. UnLearning churches will do the same. The new generation of emerging churches is connecting in deeply personal ways with real people in the churches' local communities.

On Sunday afternoon my wife, Carolyn, and I were taking a walk in our neighborhood. One of the houses we'd always liked was up for sale and had signs for an open house, so we went inside. "What kind of work do you do?" the realtor asked us. I told her I am the pastor at Ginghamsburg.

"I went to a divorce-recovery group there," she replied. By narrowcasting, we had met her at her point of felt need, in the now.

How specific can your narrowcasting be? One of our most narrowly targeted worship services at Ginghamsburg is intended specifically to meet the spiritual needs of those served by our New Path food pantry. New Path clients have access to groceries and household items, and can work with the organization to receive furniture, a car, and other financial assistance as they have need. Servants in this ministry offer prayer and guidance as they meet clients' physical needs, but through our Gateway Café worship service on Monday nights, clients also enjoy fellowship, a hearty meal, and a customized version of the previous weekend's message.

Several years ago, we discussed building a larger worship space at Ginghamsburg. Our worship attendance had been growing steadily and we were reaching our capacity at our five weekend worship celebrations. After prayerful consideration, however, we decided that Christ and our community would be better served by multiplication rather than expansion. Rather than increasing our space so that we could broadcast to more people at one time, we added services to our schedule, narrowcasting to meet more people in various ways to meet their unique needs.

We now offer more than twenty weekly services that vary in venue, focus, and style. In addition to the Gateway Café mentioned above, we offer two Next Step services, targeted at people in recovery from addiction and abuse. On Saturday nights, our main worship space is made more relaxed and intimate with tables of eight or so people, each replacing the usual rows of chairs. On Sunday morning, people worship simultaneously in two locations, meeting not just in our main worship space with its large stage, but also in Ginghamsburg Church's original nineteenth-century clapboard building a few miles up the road (our "South Campus"), which we have transformed with comfy couches and a coffee bar. On Monday nights at the South Campus, we have Worship at the ARK, a more intimate worship experience featuring Starbucks coffee and weekly Communion.

By multiplying rather than expanding, we are able to minimize bricks and maximize mission. People who are enriched by meeting with others in recovery can do so, while those who love the lights and drums of a large celebration can worship that way. People who enjoy a smaller worship setting can fellowship with others over a cup of coffee, while still more meet in House Churches, where they can have dinner together, pray, sing, and hear the week's message on DVD. This narrowcasting means I have to preach five times each weekend (thank goodness some services use the DVD!), but that use of my time and energy is well worth it to reach more people in the style and setting they connect with best.

Third-Wave Churches

Bob Buford, founder of Leadership Network, wrote a foreword to one of my previous books, *Real Followers*. In it he calls the next generation of churches "third-wave churches." They are the ones effectively reaching pre-Christian people. You've not heard of most of them yet. They're under the radar because they're under one thousand in attendance. But they represent the wave of the future.

As Buford describes it, "The first wave . . . was one of *replication*. The church in the United States started as an import from

Europe." Immigrants from Western Europe simply relocated their traditions, dogmas, methodologies, and worship styles with them as they moved. They were literally transplanted from one continent to another.

The second wave, which reached its apex around the turn of the millennium, is *proclamation*. This was born out of the first and second Great Awakenings in the United States and reached its zenith in the megachurch movement. It is based on a platform-proclaimer who gives a presentation to spectator-receivers who watch and process it. The megachurch mastered this medium through music, drama, and powerful teaching. The emphasis is on broadcast to the masses—the gathering of the crowds.

The third wave, representing the new thing God is doing, is *demonstration*. These are churches of contagious faith living out authentic biblical community expressed through compassionate service and social justice. "Christianity in this context is more pastoral and more hands-on," says Buford. "It's an anywhere and anytime connection."[2] The emphasis is not so much on gathering crowds as speaking to individuals. Not so much telling people about Christ as showing them Christ. Third-wave churches are highly personal and interactive.

UnLearning churches belong to this third wave. They narrowcast the gospel message in more focused ways for greater impact on each person. They value quality over quantity and strive to transform lives through a powerful, personal experience of God.

One Church That's UnLearning

Axxess, Arlington, Texas

www.myspace.com/axxessfellowship

- **Quick Description:** A missional community attempting to reveal the truth of Christ in one another's lives through fellowship, sharing resources, and being attentive to the needs of the cultures and communities in which we live.

- **History:** Axxess was planted in 1997 as a "church within a church" of Pantego Bible Church, and became an independent church in 2002. Axxess is now a missional group of believers meeting at the Arlington Museum of Art on Sundays, and in organically organized groups of friends throughout the week.

"We're unLearning the way we do evangelism. The gospel story must live in our lives; it dies when it is broadcast or passed without human contact. The idea of a limited being obtaining absolute truth is dead for those we are trying to reach. Truth cannot be disembodied anymore; it must be incarnated for people to embrace it. The last hundred years in the United States have seen a period of tremendous proclamation of the gospel, but the next hundred years will most likely be marked as a period of tremendous demonstration of it. We don't operate by driving our mission down through the congregation; we operate in relationships—and by the gifts we see in our people. We try to measure by the quality of our relationships; we don't measure effectiveness in typical ways. We have chosen to focus on a Central Person (the person of Christ) rather than on a central theology or a central mission.

"We recognize that the majority of Evangelicalism has become enthralled with dispensational eschatology and the idea that the world is a 'sinking ship'; with the priority on getting people into lifeboats, so much so that most congregations have literally given up on being a transformative presence in their community and culture seeking only to fill their auditoriums, believing that this is 'evangelism.' We have instead chosen to measure the success of our evangelism by observing our culture and seeing how kingdom-like or Christlike it becomes. We don't measure evangelism as how many people but rather how much kingdom: Is the crime rate down? Is beauty celebrated? Is justice present? Are the hungry fed? Is care provided to the margins of society that cannot care for themselves? etc. We believe that a church practicing evangelism will transform the culture, not just fill up an auditorium."

—Brad Cecil, Axxess Pastor since 1996; age: midforties

3

Engaging the Whole Person

God created us as multisensory beings so we can richly experience every aspect of our lives on this planet. People learn best when all their senses are engaged. The next generation of churches will avoid the stiff and cerebral and will offer people a multisensory experience of God.

I remember the first time I visited a Barnes & Noble store in Cincinnati. I immediately smelled the coffee, walked in that direction, and was surprised that they were offering it for free. Before I accepted a cup, I saw that they had a great coffee bar. So I bypassed the free stuff and bought a white chocolate cappuccino.

Then I noticed a guy playing jazz on the piano. Barnes & Noble was featuring his CDs, so I bought one.

In fact, the store carried a large music selection. It was better than the CD store in my community. It included a huge bank of listening stations. And I had entered the place thinking it was a store for books only!

I went in thinking I was on a short errand to buy a magazine about log homes. I ended up hanging out in this bookstore for a couple of hours—and I came home with a shopping bag full of CDs and books.

Stores like Barnes & Noble have become more than places to spend money; they are environments where people spend the day. Bookstores have become the new American hangout. People do far more there than buy books. They stand around and meet friends. They sit in comfortable leather chairs, drink coffee, and read books while listening to live music.

Bookstores like this are more like homes or restaurants. Libraries, by contrast, are more like churches.

All the libraries I've visited seem to specialize in hard chairs, reminding me of hard-backed pews. A pastor friend, Daryl Ward, told me, "I love being surrounded by books, but libraries are too sanitary." He's right. Libraries are too quiet, too linear, too predictable, and there's no coffee or food. They're not open late, either. Traditional libraries are stiff and institutional, they have sterile architecture, and the chairs are uncomfortable—just like those in a lot of churches.

The fundamental difference lies in their philosophy of space. Libraries and churches often think functionally, rather than environmentally. They design themselves for information, rather than experience.

Like libraries, most churches are institutions of modernity and are based on how we thought people learned. When I was a kid, my parents said, "Michael, turn off the television while you're doing your homework." So I'd put my stereo on instead. "You can't learn with music blaring," my folks would continue. "Go where it's quiet."

Compare that setting with a phone call I once received from my son while he was attending an Ivy League college. He was studying for the next day's physics midterm, chatting with friends on the Internet, playing music in the background, and talking to me—all at the same time. Yet he did much better in school than I ever hoped to do myself!

The old method was to minimize noise; the new approach is to increase stimulation. Far from the old-fashioned church service where people sat quietly to hear the pastor preach and the choir sing, today's multimedia worship engages all the senses with video, lights, surround sound, and interactive devotional experiences. Engaging people's senses does not require advanced technology, however—candles, acoustic guitar, drama, and draped fabric create an equally multisensory environment. Whatever the method and style, unLearning churches are intentional about facilitating multisensory experiences through which people can be transformed.

Experience over Commodity

Small towns are a lot like churches in their need to reinvent themselves for the needs of people today. In 1999, the last appliance store closed in one of Ohio's county-seat towns near where I live. Its proprietor died, and no one could find a future for the store. Previous closures included the last shoe store and last drugstore, both of which had relocated out of the downtown area five years before.

The mayor was convinced that the best solution was to repeat the 1950s. He felt that a replacement store, such as a new drugstore, would draw business back to town. But it hasn't happened.

By contrast, my town—Tipp City, Ohio, population six thousand—continues to reinvent itself. It is now an inviting little community, known for its antique and toy stores, deli tables on the sidewalks, and an old 1800s hotel that has been turned into a group of specialty shops. On Friday nights the streets are closed to traffic and musical groups perform. People like hanging out in downtown Tipp City because it offers more than shoes or appliances. It offers them a relaxing and enjoyable experience.

While some towns are trying to reach back and grasp the past, offering various commodities they hope people want, others move forward to reinvent themselves for the future, building a whole new environment for a postmodern experience-economy world.

Churches are doing that too. My friend Troy Dean pastors University Praise Church in Fullerton, California. He is passionate about multisensory worship that engages the senses to help people experience God. It's a far bigger issue than merely adding or removing candles, however. "Candles are not the answer to postmodern experience," he says. "Flow, connection, expression, community, safety, multifaceted learning, participation, activity, space, aesthetics with form, icons, and artifacts—all of these together are what it takes for people to experience God with all their senses engaged."

UnLearning churches realize that people become engaged through environment and experiences. Such churches develop an environment that frees people and allows them to experience God in closer and deeper ways than they've ever experienced before. Too many people believe they cannot find an experience of God in the institutional church. This is a spiritual age in which people are looking for an experience of God more than an explanation of God.

Protestant churches, especially, can default toward proclamation over experience, with worship services featuring long, boring sermons in visually bland settings. We may joke about the "smells and bells" of more liturgical traditions, but the elaborate rituals and ornate sanctuaries of old-world cathedrals grasp something that many of us in today's churches have forgotten— that scents and sounds as well as visual imagery and inviting textures are important in creating a worship experience that engages the whole person.

Many people today assume that all they'll find in church are abstract, cerebral ideas, theological definitions, and moral correction. But Jesus is God coming down to earth to serve real human needs. The message of the Incarnation is that God comes to everyday people. Like me. Like the church I serve. Like the people in my community who need an experience of God. Churches that reach people today by demonstrating radical Christianity do so by leading people to experience God, not just religious practices.

Ginghamsburg Church tries each week to help people experience God in a variety of ways. On Christmas Eve several years ago, we went further than we ever had before to help the entire Dayton community have a multisensory experience of God. "We wanted to change Christmas from an event to an experience," explains Kim Miller, Ginghamsburg's creative director. "We wanted people to feel that the heart of their Christmas was the

Ginghamsburg experience. So we created a place to bring friends and family to be part of a holiday environment and to interact with others, coming and hanging out for as long as they chose. Our desire was to create a lingering memory of their God-experience that day at Ginghamsburg."

We put flesh on these goals by creating a huge one-stop shop. We had a petting zoo, sleigh rides, a coffee shop featuring a display of works by a local artist, and a jazz band in the foyer. "These gathering points became an oasis that connected us with the awe and wonder of life," says Kim. "We knew that Christmas Eve is still the best day to bring someone to church, so we'd give them the whole nine yards when they came." People came in droves, representing almost three times our typical weekend attendance. Not only did Ginghamsburg people bring their friends, but those guests brought their friends, too.

Being in Relationship

The smell of scented candles. The sound of invigorating music. The sight of inspiring worship images. The taste of fresh-baked communion bread. All of these can help make the presence of God real to people, but none are so powerful as the caring touch of a friend. Genuine interpersonal relationships are crucial to the church's mission of bringing all people into relationship with God. Engaging the whole person means going beyond the head-sense of doctrine and theology, and even beyond the heart-sense of deeply inspirational worship, to touch the very soul of each person by being the hands and feet of Christ in an authentic community.

As part of that amazing Christmas Eve at Ginghamsburg, we introduced something called the Family Room. We used an easily accessible room upstairs from our worship area. It has a cozy atmosphere, couches, candles, and coffee tables. It became a place to meet people to talk over spiritual issues and have prayer. In our flyers that invited people to Christmas Eve, we described all the options available, including the Family Room. (We originally preferred the more user-friendly phrase "Living Room" until we discovered that the term was already in use as the name of a strip club in Dayton.)

At the end of every worship celebration, we told people that the Family Room was open, and if they had any needs to talk over or pray through, to simply make their way upstairs to the Family Room, where caring and competent people (lay pastors) were waiting to meet with them. It was a huge success. Even our professional saxophone player from Dayton who had come to play that day kept going up between sets to continue his dialogue with someone in the Family Room.

The Family Room is now an ongoing place of ministry here at Ginghamsburg. We think of it as a postmodern altar or prayer room. The traditional altar experience is challenging in a church as large as ours because people can feel herded in and out too quickly, not to mention the lack of privacy in the worship area. We have prayer rooms, but they have space for only one conversation at a time, and most people in our culture find it too intimidating to engage one-on-one with a stranger in a small room. The Family Room was a key piece of our desire to take faith beyond worship and into the everyday needs and struggles of each person.

Radical church is the power of God demonstrated through our common life together. Programs and events do not change people. We are changed by the ways we live in relationship. Radical church is God's prototype of an authentic community. We do not expect perfection from one another. Only God can give that. We look to one another to experience grace, encouragement, and accountability. We can encourage one another to become all that Christ has created us to be.

A few years ago, I watched a movement spring up at Ginghamsburg. It is a group of young heroes

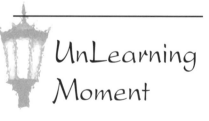

UnLearning Moment

What senses—other than hearing—could you engage to affect worshipers and seekers on multiple levels?

from ages eighteen to thirty. They call themselves The Gathering. These are young people with a sense of being called out and together. They talk with one another about where their mission needs to go. Then they make it happen as they mentor others in their age-group. They exemplify what it means to be one in heart and passion. That's what radical church looks like. Not a place, but a people.

UnLearning churches are places where people from all walks and in all stages of life can connect. The big thing of the 1990s was to have baby boomer churches, Generation X churches, and gatherings specific to other age-groups. Postmodern churches are cross-generational. Especially in this era in which families are broken and people often live far from relatives, a church family in which children and empty nesters, teenagers and the elderly can all build relationships is even more valuable.

When Ginghamsburg first launched a Saturday night worship celebration, like many others, we predicted that it would draw a crowd of singles and young families. We were wrong. There are more senior adults than young people on Saturday nights. One Saturday night, after we had just played "Higher" by the secular rock group Creed ("Can you take me higher, to the place where blind men see?"), I couldn't resist asking a seventy-five-year-old man why he was there.

"What do you mean?" he asked.

"Well, the music is loud and really contemporary," I replied.

"What kind of music do you think I listen to?" he asked in reply. I couldn't even try to venture a guess.

"When I was twenty, Elvis arrived, and when I was thirty, the Beatles hit the scene, and I liked them too," he continued. "I've been raised on contemporary music, and that's what you have here."

That older gentleman really helped me start unLearning my assumptions about various generations. One summer we invited the community to a get-acquainted event on our church campus. Our Welcome Tent featured a swing band. To our surprise, people in their seventies were dancing alongside teenagers. We sent one of our camera teams out to get people's responses to the day. One older woman summarized the significance of what we were trying to do: "It's encouraging to know that even at my age I'm not done yet. I've been in lots of churches in my life. I've encountered more changed lives here because Ginghamsburg opens its arms and doors to all kinds of people who want to find out what's going on with Jesus."

The human body is a unit. Though made of many parts, they form one body. So it is with Christ. For we were all baptized by one Spirit into one body—whether we are old or young, rich or poor, black, white, yellow, or brown. We were all given one Spirit. (See Galatians 3:27-28 and 1 Corinthians 12:12-13.) In its early days, the modern church-growth movement gave the impression that growing churches were homogeneous groupings where everyone was (or should be) alike, sporting the same skin color, economic status, and political persuasion. There's a big problem with that value. "People-just-like-me" churches are unlike the kingdom of God. Just as it is important for the church experience to connect with the whole body of each worshiper, it is important to connect with the whole body of Christ, bringing all kinds of people together.

Meaning over Activity

UnLearning churches focus more on connecting people to meaning than to activity. Fifteen years ago we would have emphasized getting people to show up for church programs and listen-and-learn meetings. We would have sponsored a seminar and gauged its success by how many attended. Now we measure success by asking, "How are people finding life change and purpose through the experience?" People are not looking for church meetings so much as for life meaning. We want to know if their church experience makes a difference in their relationships, parenting skills, Christian witness, and stewardship.

This paradigm translates into the organization's structure as well. Older-mind-set churches usually require a lot of committees and meetings. Ginghamsburg finds that its people have neither the time nor the patience for multiple committee activities, so we are down to one committee of nine people called the

Leadership Board. No more staff-parish, missions, or finance committees. Major businesses operate with one board, but too often tiny churches become immobilized by layers of committees. They spend hours debating what color carpeting to put in the church narthex, or the precise wording of the congregation's statement of beliefs.

Today's marketing gurus understand that today's culture isn't looking for information about products. Just how much could you write down about a Nike shoe after watching one television ad about it? Today's culture isn't looking to understand. Nike commercials don't talk about or even show athletic apparel. Instead, they offer a thirty-second experience.

The church could learn something from Nike. People don't want information about your religion—what people really want is a life-altering experience. UnLearning churches understand that. It's not about policies and procedures, or even morality and ideology. It's about relationships. It's about creating environments where people can experience God.

One Church That's UnLearning

Seacoast Church, Campuses in South Carolina, North Carolina, Georgia, and on the Internet
www.seacoast.org

- **Quick Description:** One Church in Many Locations.
- **History:** Nondenominational. Started in 1988 by Greg Surratt, and has grown to include 12 campuses across South Carolina, North Carolina, and Georgia.

- **Attendance:** 9,000 in 26 services.

"Imagine you are a young adult and you have been visiting church for a few weekends. You have started to come to church because you feel like something is missing, and it seems like there is a puzzle piece here, but you are not quite sure what to do about it. You listen to the message and it seems that God would have you 'do' something. But what?

"For most of my life, the typical model of worship was to sing a few songs, make a few announcements, and then hear a message from scripture. Many times there would be one song at the end of the message that we called a 'song of invitation,' but as far as a real opportunity to respond, there was little to none. What if there was a time to 'do' something, to respond physically to what had happened in your heart during the worship or the message?

"In 2006, our senior pastor, Greg Surratt, noticed that after the message, people were dealing with what God had done in their hearts and minds and the encounter with the power and presence of God they had experienced, but were left with only a 'See you next week!' That was the weekend that everything changed at Seacoast. We unLearned and reLearned how to respond to God. With a fusion of the past and the present, we now see believers responding to God in a highly experiential, yet historically beautiful way, and unbelievers responding to explore Christ. During this time of three songs of response, people have an opportunity to sing songs of worship, write down their sins and pin them to a cross, light a candle as a symbol of prayer, pray with an elder, and take Communion with fellow believers. We call it holy chaos as people get up out of their seats to 'do' something in response to God."
—Shawn Wood, Experiences Pastor, has been with the church since 2001; age: early thirties

4 Thriving in Paradox

The church of the last five hundred years has lived in an "either-or" world called modernity. The postmodern church embraces the "both-and" of paradox, where two seemingly contradictory attitudes exist at the same time, and where it's okay not to know for sure.

Jesus taught that his life mission would take him to a cruel and painful death and then he would rise from the dead. His first followers recognized the importance of his coming back to life. "If Christ has not been raised, then our proclamation has been in vain and your faith has been in vain," said the Apostle Paul (1 Corinthians 15:14).

The paradox of the "living dead" is still with us today. Jesus' followers must experience the presence of the one who came out of the tomb. We are to consider ourselves "dead to sin and alive to God in Christ Jesus" (Romans 6:11). Jesus' death and resurrection created a huge paradox, where two seemingly contradictory things existed at the same time. Remember, empty tombs don't make sense. We can't prove the Resurrection rationally.

The church of the last five hundred years has lived in an "either-or" world called modernity, ever since the invention of the printing press and the dawning of the Enlightenment. The modern church has tried to master the art of explanation. Its love affair with tight logic and ordered reasons for faith has seriously downplayed the paradoxes in Jesus' teaching and in the church he created. Can logic ever really explain how our Savior can be completely God and completely human at the same time? We have much unLearning to do.

The modern understanding of the universe reigned until the 1970s and 1980s, when people's worldviews began to enter a time of revolutionary change. We no longer call today's period the modern era but the postmodern era—a time when people have "gotten over" the total reliance on empirical evidence and are far more eager to live in paradox and mystery.

It doesn't make sense to live out of only the cerebral part of our beings. God created us with far more complexity. We are people of mystery who live in a creation of mystery and serve a God of mystery.

The postmodern church, like the premodern church in which Christianity was born, lives in the "both-and" of paradox. The emerging church celebrates mystery more than explanation.

For the leaders of tomorrow's church, this world of paradox represents an ancient-future church. It is stained glass *and* media screens. It is candles *and* stage lights. It is secular *and* sacred. Former pastor and futurologist Bill Easum predicts that "worship will become more Eastern and more high tech. . . . The issue is no longer is it contemporary or is it traditional. Now, does it have spirit? Does it have the mystery of the east and the high-tech of the west? Can it say it all with words? If so, it has missed the point."[1]

Both High-Tech and High-Touch

The practical application of Easum's observation is that emerging churches are *both* high-tech *and* high-touch. It may seem paradoxical that the Internet has made social interactions much less reliant on face-to-face encounters, and yet has cultivated vast social networks of people who may never meet in person but who nonetheless form real friendships. The church is the same way. Through technology, churches can invite the outside world, far beyond their church doors, to participate in their personal quest for God.

Many times each year, Ginghamsburg sends a camera team to a nearby town—Dayton, Columbus, or Cincinnati. We ask such questions as "What is hard about faith?" and "Why do you—or don't you—go to church?" Then we edit the responses into a short video that we use as part of our worship celebrations, designed around a particular theme.[2] Sometimes we recognize friends or coworkers in these "on the street" video shots. This method increases the variety of perspectives represented in worship, and enhances our cultural relevance.

UnLearning Moment

What is one high-tech element your church has embraced? How can it be used as a high-touch tool?

Secular media has been making a similar transition in recent years. Consider the evolution Ginghamsburg's creative director Kim Miller observed between Johnny Carson and Jay Leno. On the earlier *Tonight Show*, the talent was limited to Johnny Carson, Ed McMahon, the current guest, and occasionally the bandleader. The twenty-first–century version of *The Tonight Show* with Jay Leno lets the entire audience become the cast, along with the camera people, directors, band, and even tourists and locals on the street near the studio. *The Late Show with David Letterman* and other late-night talk shows do the same thing. They are accomplishing a high-touch experience with extremely high-tech tools.

UnLearning churches maximize technology for the purpose of telling stories that connect people to an experience of God, authentic community, and life purpose.

Ginghamsburg embraces technology and excellence, but never for the purpose of presentation alone. We use the storytelling abilities of technology, along with a passion for excellence, for the purpose of more effectively connecting people with an experience of God. It maximizes participation. As Kim Miller explains:

> Gone are the days when even church folks could listen to one or two people (better known as talking heads). Now, using technology, the world can become our "cast." . . . Suddenly we're not just imagining what we think people are feeling on a subject, but we have the real deal to watch and listen to. Participation goes to a whole new level. High-tech serves high-touch.[3]

When the *Wall Street Journal* wanted to study how technology has changed the way people attend church, it profiled Ginghamsburg. A reporter interviewed people about their experience of our worship celebrations. She noted that high-tech worship celebration is more than saying, "Let us pray, watch movies, and listen to a killer band." We experience highly personalized media pieces connected with prayer, music, and interaction. She noted that additional high-touch occurs at Ginghamsburg through more than two hundred adult cell groups and through online personalized fellowship communities on our website.[4]

The Internet allows unLearning churches to be *both* local *and* global. People might be more connected to the church where they log on than the church they attend. We know of many people who live in other parts of the world who may be affiliated with another church, but for whom the primary source of their God experience is Ginghamsburg. One lady in Australia e-mailed us, asking if we could tweak the layout of our website so that it would print more cleanly for her. She explained, "I download messages and print them from 'my church' "—referring to Ginghamsburg—"to give them to the people in my neighborhood"—referring to her friends eleven thousand miles from Ohio!

Mike Gibbs, a former member of Ginghamsburg, moved to Florida several years ago and is active in a church there. However, he's continued as an unofficial leader of our Internet-based fellowship online community, designed for people who want to chat about Ginghamsburg's weekly message—which is available in streaming video, text format, and podcast. Like them, he experiences the sermons on the Internet. When people ask for help understanding our worship celebrations or my sermons, Mike explains them better than I could. Yet he doesn't even attend Ginghamsburg in person anymore!

Seeing technology and intimacy as polar opposites would have rendered us irrelevant in today's digital age. Embracing this paradox, however, has helped us to thrive in our ministry to a twenty-first-century generation.

Unity in Diversity

Just as seemingly impersonal technology brings people together in surprising ways, other paradoxes of the unLearning church unite people even as they embrace diverse, seemingly contradictory perspectives.

In today's polarized political arena, it is significant that postmodern churches are politically *both* conservative *and* liberal. I've been at Ginghamsburg nearly thirty years, and even longtimers don't know whether I vote Republican or Democrat. I like to irritate both sides! Churches too often build themselves around ideas and causes, such as political parties. In Jesus' day, the Pharisees believed in everything and more, while the Sadducees believed in nothing and less. Jesus was neither. The emerging leader is neither. The gospel doesn't toe any party line.

At a recent conference sponsored by Ginghamsburg, participants came from some thirty different denominational groups and ten different countries. A hundred years ago, our focus would have been on our differences, and we would not have met together. Today, members of a theologically conservative denomination might not even know or care that they are worshiping and learning alongside representatives from denominations on the other side of the spectrum. Instead, they focus on the commonality of our faith and commitment to Jesus Christ.

We did a quick survey one weekend and found that more than nine hundred people who attend Ginghamsburg (a United Methodist church) view their primary religious identity as Roman Catholic! Many go to Mass as well as participate with us in the same weekend. I'm glad people don't feel like they have to choose between denominations, because postmodern churches are *both* Catholic *and* evangelical.

We've offered liturgical Ash Wednesday worship celebrations in recent years, and find they draw both people from all over the community. Many already have ashes on their foreheads, indicating they have already been to Mass or perhaps to an Episcopal service that day.

"For centuries, the one sure way to tell a Catholic from a Protestant was to look for the dark smudge on the forehead on Ash Wednesday," began a *Boston Globe* article on changes in religious observances. "No more. Reflecting an increasing demand for ritual and decreasing hostility toward Catholicism among Protestants, a growing number of Protestant churches today will be offering worshipers the traditional sign of penitence and mourning."

" 'Five-hundred years ago we gave up these rituals because we didn't want to be Catholic, and now we're saying there was a loss for us spiritually,' said Susan P. Dickerman of the Massachusetts Conference of the United Church of Christ. 'There's a tremendous yearning for developing spirituality.' "[5]

We teach that a person comes into relationship with God through faith. "As it is written, 'The one who is righteous will live by faith' " (Romans 1:17b). We emphasize, as did John Wesley, the gift of grace: "For by grace you have been saved through faith, and this is not your own doing; it is the gift of God—not the result of works" (Ephesians 2:8-9a). And we welcome people from all faith backgrounds to come alongside us in Christ, whether their heritage is Protestant, Catholic, Orthodox, or something else.

UnLearning churches also welcome nonbelievers to participate in the worship celebration. The church is for *both* seekers *and* saints together. Imitating the most popular church-growth models of the 1980s and 1990s, many churches offered special services designed to be "seeker-friendly," while saving the tough stuff for those who were already believers. Today's churches are becoming both believer-focused and seeker-focused at the same time. It's like the parable where Jesus says to go into the streets and invite *everyone* to God's party: " 'The wedding is ready, but those invited were not worthy. Go therefore into the main streets, and invite everyone you find to the wedding banquet.' Those slaves went out into the streets and gathered all whom they found, both good and bad; so the wedding hall was filled with guests" (Matthew 22:8b-10). God's kingdom is a paradox in which both believers and seekers are called together at the same time.

The people who had the hardest time catching on to this vision of the kingdom were the Pharisees. Jesus condemned the religious leaders for locking people out of the "party" when they weren't even experiencing the party themselves! God's word for us today is "Don't shut the door to my party!" Or as Jesus explained elsewhere, the good wheat and the bad weeds will grow together until God separates them later at harvesttime (see Matthew 13:24-28).

Some people accuse next-generation churches of dumbing down the gospel to appeal to everyone. But isn't that God's intent? When the infinite God becomes finite and puts it on a level where I can get it, the proper term to use is "dumbing down." God dumbed it down without watering it down. The gospel is offensive, but we need to put it in a language so that people recognize that they've been offended!

The Joy of Not Knowing

The gospel is offensive because it goes so far beyond what we would consider rational. Jesus is both human and divine? Save your life by losing it? Sell everything you have and give it to the poor? These things may not make much sense to us, but they are part of what makes the Christian life so amazing.

The church of my childhood was consumed with giving the right answers. Churches of tomorrow focus on asking the right questions.

Asking questions of his followers and even his detractors was Jesus' most-used method of teaching. When the Pharisees tried to trap him by asking whether it was right to pay taxes to Caesar, Jesus responded by taking the coin and asking "Whose portrait and inscription are on it?" (Luke 20:26).

Even when he was being interrogated by Pontius Pilate, and was asked point-blank, "Are you the King of the Jews?" he did not give a clear answer. Instead, he asked Pilate, "Do you ask this on your own, or did others tell you about me?" (John 18:33-34).

People like me want clear answers. If I had been alive during Jesus' earthly ministry, I would have pressed him hard to get the inside scoop on who he was. "Come on, Jesus," I'd have said, "I have my notebook open and pen ready. Please cut to the chase and tell me who you are."

But Jesus answered questions with questions: "Who do *you* say that I am?" (Matthew 16:15, emphasis added).

We often think life could be easier if we could only receive clear and immediate answers. Jesus, on the other hand, understood that real growth happens as we struggle with significant questions, when we can have the safe emotional space to do so without judgment. If people aren't free to ask hard questions, they may never get the real answers that they need. I am unLearning the habit of giving quick answers.

People often assume that having "faith like a child" (see Mark 10:13-15) means naively trusting and never doubting. But children never blindly accept what someone tells them! They are always questioning and always curious. I asked Sherry Douglas, who directed our children's ministries at Ginghamsburg for many years, how many questions the average child asks in

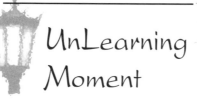

UnLearning Moment

What honest questions do you imagine people want to ask? Are your worship, classroom, and fellowship settings safe spaces to explore these questions?

a day. She estimated more than one hundred. Some parents would say their toddlers ask three hundred a day! By the time we are middle-aged adults, however, the average is down to a handful of significant questions a day. As we grow older, we have a tendency to lose our inquiring sense of awe and wonder. We forget how to be childlike, and we begin to equate questioning with a lack of faith.

Questioning, seeking people are not without faith. And they are not without God. Culture today can be relativistic, but it is not anti-god. People today believe in God, gods, and goddesses—they just don't know which one is real. Today's post-Christian spirituality is one that rejects absolutes and intolerance. It is a spirituality with no biblical concepts. It sees Christianity's claim of exclusivity as unacceptable— evidence of close-mindedness. Yet Jesus said, "I am the way, the truth, and the life. No one comes to the Father except through me" (John 14:6). The early church affirmed that "there is no other name under heaven given among mortals by which we can be saved" (Acts 4:12b).

But Jesus' motive in teaching was not so that we could argue others into becoming his followers. Jesus said, "I am giving you these commands so that you may love one another" (John 15:17). Christlike love creates an environment in which people feel safe to question, seek, and grow.

Safe Space to Ask Hard Questions

UnLearning churches must be environments of trust. They must create safe spaces where the Spirit can work through people's inquiring quests for God. They welcome people who don't give or have all the "right" answers. They invite people to ask honest questions without chastising folks for struggling with the answers. They create communities of grace-space, allowing seekers the freedom to deal with the deepest questions of their hearts.

Through their own honesty, congregational leaders can demonstrate that the church is a safe space for questioning. When leaders are transparent in the questions they are asking, they gain credibility and authenticity with those looking to them for spiritual guidance. How am I as a pastor supposed to tell you what to believe when I don't have all the answers either? I was once spiritually blind. Jesus opened my eyes and made me see. He was resurrected from the grave and changed my life. But there are many days when I still pray, "I believe; help my unbelief." In fact, it's one of my most frequent prayers.

In her book, *Traveling Mercies: Some Thoughts on Faith*, Anne Lamott describes how she found a church that was a safe place for her. As the reader experiences the narrative of her life journey, with its earthy language, painful failures, and times of confusion and disillusionment, there is no doubting that her faith is real. She has invited the God of Jesus Christ to invade her life, and she credits her church as a people who accepted her when she was pregnant and unwed, as a place that continues to welcome her to ask hard questions.

My friend Scott Parsons, on a similar journey but a different road, makes connections for me. In 1998, at age fifty-one, he came to Ginghamsburg for the first time. During his third year with us, he made a faith commitment to be a Jesus follower. He did this in a community that's striving to connect people to an experience of God, a community that lives in paradox, and that provides a safe environment to ask critical questions.

Here is what Scott says about his Jesus journey:

I guess I'm still a seeker and always will be—but by way of a very convoluted path, I have come to a point of referring to myself as "tentatively Christian." I got to this point by translating the essential vocabulary of Christians into meanings I could embrace. It has worked well enough that now I rarely feel the need to translate.

When I thinking of a church setting out to make an appeal to a seeker like me—knowing my own attitudes and resistances—I'm very impressed that they'd even try. It seems to me like what they're doing is similar to adopting children who have highly limiting and irreversible challenges and conditions—the kind only a miracle can overcome.

For people like me, actions completely drown out words. Behavior—Christian behavior—is the only thing that will win us. There's nothing more persuasive in the human range of acts. A brave "seeker church" operates on the certainty that God is much too great to be threatened by a seeker's wild questions or unconventional speculation. It wasn't arguments that ultimately made God real for me. I think it was the gradual turning of my attention toward

God—something that happened because of Ginghamsburg Church. I had to be listening to hear God.

As a seeker, what have I been seeking? It has never been salvation or heaven. I'm not really interested in those wonderful gifts, although I won't refuse them if they are offered. What I wanted was an encounter with a real God, someone who can take me higher.

That encounter began for me one ordinary day when my mind was relaxed and I suddenly realized that I knew that God was present around me. As for Jesus, I am still trying to understand him. I place faith in the idea that if I love Jesus enough, belief will fall to the side. And I do love Jesus.

Scott Parsons is someone who asks lots of questions, and I hear God through Scott's life. Scott came to Ginghamsburg as a self-described agnostic, although his attendance has been better than that of many members. After a long period of critical questioning in a safe environment, he declared that he is a tentative follower of Jesus—a work in progress.

Imagine a people who live in an environment of grace and unconditional love. Imagine a safe space where we can be honest enough to work on our "stuff." In this place we find the freedom to tell the truth of who we really are on the inside. We can move out of fear and into trust. We can begin to truly live and to make a difference in God's created purpose, empowered to leave the safe spaces to practice authentic love in the dangerous places of life.

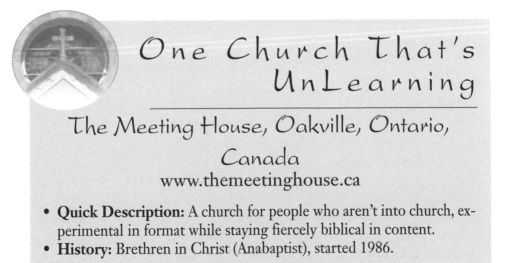

One Church That's UnLearning

The Meeting House, Oakville, Ontario, Canada
www.themeetinghouse.ca

- **Quick Description:** A church for people who aren't into church, experimental in format while staying fiercely biblical in content.
- **History:** Brethren in Christ (Anabaptist), started 1986.

- **Attendance:** 4,000+, spread out over multiple sites linked by live satellite teaching.

"We include a question-and-answer period as part of our Sunday teaching each week. In today's culture we're encouraged to ask questions in grade school, high school, college, and university, but then we invite people to learn at church and expect them to be quiet, passive receivers of truth. Our ongoing challenge is to find ways of keeping our Sunday services open and interactive even as attendance grows. Our 'Q & Eh?' time (hey, we're Canadians) is the part of the teaching that many people most look forward to and tell others about. Even if only a minority of people have the chance to ask a question, the fact that we demonstrate an openness to questions immediately demonstrates our emphasis on dialogue, integrity, and vulnerability. Our midweek small groups (called Home Churches) then give people a further opportunity to share their opinions and interact with the biblical material since these groups focus on the topic of Sunday's teaching."

—Bruxy Cavey, teaching pastor and author of *The End of Religion*, has been with the church since 1996; age: early forties

5 A Culture of Reckless Love

The world doesn't need religious organizations, but communities that are willing to live boldly and passionately, to step outside their comfort zones to serve those in need. UnLearning churches guide people along their spiritual journey by demonstrating Christ's reckless love for the world.

When Jesus first met some of his potential disciples, he found them fishing close to the shore. Shallow waters are safe and predictable. Shoreline work is logical and risk-free.

As Jesus spoke to them about their fishing tactics, he was in essence saying to them, "You will never become the person God created you to be if you hang out here where it is safe and pre-dictable. If you are going to maximize this incredible gift of life that God has given you, you have to cast out to dangerous places. You've got to go out there to the deep spots." (See Luke 5:1-11.)

This depth and risk are part of what it means to be a follower of Jesus. Giving one's life over to God requires a lifestyle of po-tential unpredictability, out in deeper waters, yet we spend most of our lives working hard to keep things safe and under control. That's how many of our parents and grandparents in the post–World War II generation define success—working hard to create security and comfort with minimal risk. People today might change jobs and move to other towns more often than preceding generations, but that doesn't mean we're any braver when it comes to the uncertainties of life. We find ways to make a living, but we don't know how to live. There is a big difference between the two!

We do the same thing with religion. We want a god we can tame and define—who will make life safe and predictable. So we come up with little gods that fit into nice, neat categories. But God is not tame. Predictability and faith in Jesus cannot coexist.

Jesus was a lawbreaker. He did everything that you weren't supposed to do. Mark 2:1–3:6 gives a snapshot of Jesus' unpredictability. He didn't fit the definition of what religious people thought he ought to be. He ate at the wrong houses. He hung out with prostitutes, thieves, and scoundrels. He broke religious rules. He didn't fit into people's simplistic equations of what religion—or their anticipated Messiah—was supposed to look like. That's why he was rejected.

When Jesus went into a town and pulled off an amazing miracle, people would ask him to leave. People quickly saw that Jesus would disrupt their normal life patterns, as well as the social, religious, and economic norms of their culture. He would do things like curse a fig tree, drive pigs off a cliff, or turn over money-changers' tables. Who would let this man influence their children? If Jesus came into our congregations today, he wouldn't pass most churches' requirements to teach children's Sunday school. In fact, he would more likely be accepted in a biker bar than by most people in churches.

When you become infected by the risen Christ, you too will create a tension in your surrounding culture. You simply won't be able to help it. Many of us would prefer that Jesus just comfort us and bring calm and quiet to our communities, but that is not the case. Instead, Jesus brings us the courage to step out of our comfort zone and serve him with reckless abandon.

Holy Discomfort

If we want to feel comfortable and stress-free, we should go to the beach, the park, or a spa—not the church. Walking with God is not about being comfortable or having an easy life. The true follower of Jesus does not live in the middle of the herd, safe and protected, but out on the edge, in total dependence on God.

People grow the most in times of tension, adversity, and crisis, when they are struggling and wrestling with the hard questions. If we still have the same understanding of Jesus we had twenty years ago, we are probably not growing. God is the same yesterday, today, and tomorrow (see Hebrews 13:8), but our understanding and discovery of God grow and deepen. This maturity happens if we allow ourselves to remain in places of discomfort.

Our leadership team at Ginghamsburg jokes that I have the spiritual gift of irritation, and I'm proud of that! I do feel called to be a source of irritation to lives that are safe and predictable. We don't grow when we're comfortable. A pearl is formed from a grain of sand that becomes an irritant in the shell of an oyster. UnLearning churches must be this kind of irritant, afflicting the comfortable so that they may go out and comfort the afflicted.

In the second book of C. S. Lewis's *Chronicles of Narnia* series, *The Lion, the Witch and the Wardrobe*, four British children magically enter the land of Narnia and soon hear about Aslan, a lion who represents Jesus in Lewis's tale. The children are frightened to hear from Mr. and Mrs. Beaver that Aslan is a lion, and ask if he is tame. One of the little girls, Susan, declares, "I shall feel rather nervous about meeting a lion."

"That you will, dearie, and no mistake," said Mrs. Beaver. "If there's anyone who can appear before Aslan without their knees knocking, they're either braver than most or else just silly."

"Then he isn't safe?" said Lucy.

"Safe?" said Mr. Beaver. "Don't you hear what Mrs. Beaver tells you? . . . 'Course he isn't safe. But he's good. He's the King."

I am unLearning the idea that safe is best. Too many Christians today are without passion because we have made Jesus, the Lion of Judah, safe, predictable, and logical. But lions are

60

not tame, and Jesus is not predictable. So, we Christians are not called to be predictable or safe either—but we are called to be good. We are called to show God's endless and abundant love to the world, unencumbered by concern for our own safety or security.

One area in which Christians tend to err on the "safe" side rather than on the "good" side is in their giving. Too many people live recklessly when it comes to buying on credit and accruing massive debts, but suddenly get quite conservative when it comes to generous giving. I meet many people struggling to get out of debt who assume they should refrain from tithing until they are financially free. But, as I emphasize in my book *Money Matters: Financial Freedom for All God's Children*, God's economics are not like ours. God blesses our willingness to trust him with our finances, and calls us to be responsible in our spending so that we can love recklessly with our giving to him.

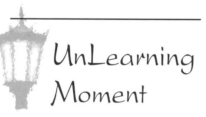

UnLearning Moment

What is one way you have created a moment of "holy discomfort" that will inspire people to do great things for God and the world?

In the past few years, Ginghamsburg has been active in offering aid to those orphaned and impoverished by civil war in the Sudan. Each Christmas, we encourage people to cut what they normally spend on Christmas in half—and give an equal amount to our Christmas Miracle Offering. Since 2005, we have collected close to $3 million for water, schools, and sustainable agriculture in Darfur, all because of people's willingness to make radical sacrifices to do good in places that need our help most.

Many people equate safety and goodness, thinking that by being reserved in their behavior, they are honoring God. To the contrary, being made in the image of a good God means risking insecurity and discomfort to show his love to the world.

Reckless Love

Love is the essence of who God is. The Bible says God is love. (See 1 John 4:8, 16.) This kind of eternal, sacrificial love is often lost on people today, even in the church. Love today can mean anything from "I crave chocolate cake," to "I must have that bike," to "I get goose bumps when I talk to you." Jesus clarifies his definition of love when he says, "This is what I mean by love. When you love, love others as I have loved you." (See John 15:12.)

Jesus came to earth because God loved us with reckless abandon. It's a love beyond self-preservation. "For God so loved the world that he gave his only Son, so that everyone who believes in him may not perish but may have eternal life" (John 3:16).

The Incarnation means that God became a man in the person of Jesus. You could even say that God was obsessed with love and passion over losing us. How obsessed? God became a human being, came after us, and was even willing to die on a cross. God showed us a go-for-broke, willing-to-be-hung-out-there, with-everything-you've-got kind of passion, without regard for his own life or limb. That's God's love for you and me. That's the love we are called to embody.

Being a Christian is not about articulating a correct doctrinal perspective, wagging a finger at those who don't conform to our way of thinking, or staying home on Saturday nights. How did Jesus say people would know who his disciples were? By how many times a month they serve or receive Communion? By the wearing of clergy robes and vestments? By seminary degrees? By bumper stickers or offices adorned with Jesus plaques? No. By the way we love one another.

A religion editor from a local newspaper came to interview me about a conference we were having at Ginghamsburg. At the end of the interview, I asked if she went to church. I assumed she did, given her line of work, but she said, "No, I am a Buddhist. I was raised in the church, but about ten years ago, I became involved in Buddhism because the highest value of Buddhism is the value of compassion."

Her next comment made me feel as if she had put her hand in my chest and squeezed my heart. "The people I grew up around in the church were some of the least compassionate people I ever knew," she added. Ouch.

Jesus is compassion made visible—the highest demonstration of compassion possible. If this organization I am connected to is not about compassion, grace, and hope, then it is not truth. We who have encountered the resurrected Christ can demonstrate unconditional love because we have experienced it. If the church fails to demonstrate that love, something is terribly wrong.

Jesus didn't say to live in his religion. He said to live in his love! You and I are to be the embodiment of God's love. The apostles teach us to "love one another, because love is from God; everyone who loves is born of God and knows God. . . . Since God loved us so much, we also ought to love one another. No one has ever seen God; if we love one another, God lives in us, and his love is perfected in us" (1 John 4:7, 11-12). The church is called to be a demonstration of God's presence in the world. It's through the demonstration of God's love that people will be able to see hope and peace in a world of chaos and isolation.

Into the Wild

Jesus was raised in a religious family. He learned the scriptures and journeyed with his parents to Jerusalem for Passover. There were times of danger and insecurity—like when his family fled to Egypt soon after his birth in order to protect him from King Herod (see Matthew 2:13-23)—but we can generally assume he enjoyed the comfort of a loving family and a close-knit community of faith. However, look what happened abruptly after Jesus' baptism: "The Spirit immediately drove him out into the wilderness. He was in the wilderness forty days, tempted by Satan; and he was with the wild beasts; and the angels waited on him" (Mark 1:12-13). The Spirit that on an earlier occasion appeared as a gentle dove now forced Jesus out into the wild where doves were replaced by vultures. Satan and wild beasts became Jesus' companions, yet angels protected him. Satan tested him, but Jesus was able to stand up to the temptation because he had a clear sense of God's calling and power in his life.

If you are a parent, you understand the daunting task of preparing your children to head out into the world. The challenge is to equip and empower them to not avoid or hide from the wild things of the world, but to face them boldly, and to demonstrate God's love in the dark places.

When Carolyn and I took our son, Jonathan, for campus visits at colleges that were talking to him about baseball scholarships, we stayed at local motels while Jonathan went off to live with the baseball players and get a feel for campus life. When we would see him the next morning, he always looked thoroughly tired.

At one place, he stayed up until three in the morning. I asked him if students were doing a lot of drinking, and he said, "Yep, it's amazing. There were four kegs of beer for the legs of a Ping-Pong table." I asked him if they stocked any soft drinks or other alternatives to alcohol. "No, all they had was beer," he said. He told me about one girl who was passed out, drunk, with vomit everywhere, and how he had to make sure she was okay.

I told Jonathan, "This is what we prepared you for. Life is not about staying in the safe places. Ginghamsburg has been a good place for you to grow up, but now you're getting kicked out. You were baptized and you took mission trips. Now God will lead you out, and wild beasts will be your companions. Jonathan, these dangerous places are the space where we proclaim and demonstrate the good news of God."

Being a pastor is similar to being a parent, in some ways. Leaders of unLearning churches are charged with preparing their congregations to head out from the safe space of the church into a world in desperate need of God's love. They must demonstrate that faith in the God of the universe means being uncomfortable, having your life turned upside down and inside out for the sake of God, following the Spirit into the dangerous and unpredictable places of life.

This is the ultimate challenge for pastors, in that it is much harder to inspire people to trust an unpredictable Spirit and love a dangerous world than it is to simply dictate beliefs. But look at Jesus' words in John 15:9-10: "As the Father has loved me, so I

64 have loved you; abide in my love. If you keep my commandments, you will abide in my love, just as I have kept my Father's commandments and abide in his love." Jesus' command doesn't say anything about belief. Rather, it is our passions that determine our actions in life, and passions are tied to our ultimate love, not our intellectual beliefs.

Jesus goes on to say, "I have said these things to you so that my joy may be in you, and that your joy may be complete. This is my commandment, that you love one another as I have loved you" (John 15:11-12).

Jesus is calling your church not to religious belief but to an affair of the heart. This world doesn't need another institutional religion that goes out and tells people what to do and what to believe. What Jesus is building and forming is a culture of reckless love. Help him lead your church to that place.

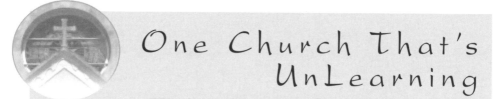

One Church That's UnLearning

Redeemer Presbyterian Church
Manhattan, New York
http://www.redeemer.com/

- **Quick Description:** A church seeking to renew the city socially, spiritually, and culturally.
- **History:** Presbyterian Church in America, started in 1989.
- **Worship Attendance:** 3,000 in 5 services.

"If Jesus were living here in New York City, with its large homosexual community, what would he be doing? For Redeemer, this simple question led to a radical unLearning: We should have a ministry to people with AIDS. So we created i58, partnering with our Greenwich Village–based church plant, The Village Church. With Isaiah 58:10-11 as our guiding scripture, volunteers from Redeemer and The Village Church cook and serve Sunday dinners at the Bailey-Holt House, a housing and resource center for homeless people living with AIDS, including some of New York's longest-living people with AIDS. Showing concern to a physically and spiritually broken community has also opened doors to share the gospel, and by request of the residents, Redeemer now holds worship services at the Bailey-Holt House twice a month. More than one person has commented, 'I've noticed a big difference in your volunteers—you actually care about people. You don't treat us like charity cases,' and 'Our clients want you back.'"

—Ron Koustas, leader of the Isaiah 58 Project
from 1994 to 2003; age: late forties

PART TWO

unLearning
Leadership

MAKING THE
VISION A
REALITY

6 Radical Prayer

UnLearning leaders are charged by God with the spiritual welfare of a group of people. They must operate out of an intuitive sense of God's direction. Radical prayer is the crucial first step to not only hearing God's direction, but acting on it.

Real change and transformation for individuals and congregations comes through commitment to radical prayer—prayer that brings us into intimate awareness of God's presence, that enables us to sense the will of God and do it. The passions and practices of unLearning churches described in earlier chapters would be meaningless if not carried out in conjunction with God's expressed vision for church. Without an intuitive sense of direction discovered through prayerful communication with God, we will not grow as individuals or as leaders of God's church.

In the hectic pace of ministry, it's easy to anesthetize our need to intimately connect with God, or to reduce our prayer time to a routine that grows meaningless over time. Real prayer is not some simple little rhyme or incantation. Cute, churchy definitions and formulas will only trivialize it. It is a deep, relational connection with God, going much deeper than the little nod-to-God kind of spiritual aerobics that a lot of us habitually fall into.

Sometimes I have Big Mac attacks in which I get a food pictured in my mind and can't get it out. I've gotten out of bed at night to fix myself a pastrami sandwich. I go to bed thinking I'll have one for lunch the next day, and then can't wait. My body is craving a certain food, and I act on that desire.

We actually have a deeper longing—an intimate, connective need for the presence of God. Just as our bodies crave food, our spirits long to be fed. Only an intimate relationship with God can fill that spiritual hunger.

A few years ago, when I spent some time in the Himalayas, I heard this expression: "When the explorer is ready, the guide will come." Prayer is our willingness to connect with the guide. Everything Jesus does is dependent on his relationship with the Father. Jesus told people, "The Son can do nothing on his own, but only what he sees the Father doing; for whatever the Father does, the Son does likewise" (John 5:19b). Before he began his public ministry, he spent forty days communing with God through prayer and fasting, demonstrating to God that he was ready for the great task ahead. When we come to that place in our spiritual journey, the transformation is indescribable, and we discover God's power in a way we have never experienced before.

For years, Wendy and her husband, Roger, had wanted a baby. They went to doctors who specialized in fertility. They did everything they could think of with no results. One evening when they were visiting in our home, we decided to pray about their need. We stood around Wendy and prayed for her. Three weeks later she found out she was pregnant with twins.

God's answers aren't always so obvious or straightforward. Sometimes God will answer a prayer like that by opening up some wonderful opportunities through adoption. Either way, God hears and knows the longings of our hearts, and wants to guide us to a place of fulfillment. Jesus said, "If you abide in me, and my words abide in you, ask for whatever you wish, and it will be done for you" (John 15:7). What a promise! What a God!

An Intimate Connection with God

Have you ever felt that your issues were not significant enough for God's involvement—that God deals only with big things? "If people are starving all over the world, how can God possibly care about my bad hair days?" you might wonder. Yet the Bible bears the claim that God knows how many hairs are left on my head and even cares if a little bird falls out of its nest.

I am unLearning my relationship with God, and discovering that God wants to be intimately involved in the details of my life. God waits to be invited into my personal spaces. The Psalms describe how David longed for such an intimate experience of God. "O God, you are my God, I seek you, my soul thirsts for you; my flesh faints for you, as in a dry and weary land where there is no water" (Psalm 63:1). What David says is that ultimately our deepest longing, our real hunger, the intimacy we crave is an intimate connectedness to God.

Prayer leads us to that intimate connectedness.

Prayer is thinking and moving with God, straining forward, like a person committed to the rigorous exercise of mountaineering. Climbing is an ongoing process of making commitments and moving forward. You have to take one foothold at a time, one handhold at a time, and then the next, and the next, and the next. To get off a plateau in any area of your life, you must make a true commitment to move forward.

During the Lenten season of 2000, I did something I'd never done before. I went into a forty-day season of fasting, excluding Sundays. God wanted to do a new thing in my life personally, and I knew that fasting would be crucial for me to discover it. It was a limited fast, but I am convinced that many spiritual benefits came as a result of that time of seeking God, including a clearer picture of what God wanted to do at Ginghamsburg. That picture will (and must) change over time—that's why it is crucial to stay in touch with God through daily prayer, so you will know when and how your focus must change.

If you watch life through human perception alone, and if you listen only to the fury of the storm, you'll stop, paralyzed with fear. When the Holy Spirit in you develops a heart-based relationship with God, you listen with the ears of your heart and see through the eyes of your heart. That's when miracles happen.

Less Talking, More Listening

Sometimes on Monday, our day off, Carolyn and I sit in the kitchen in the morning and drink coffee. I read the newspaper, and we talk. One day she was trying to tell me about her mom's current state of health. Right in the middle of Carolyn's recounting her conversation with her mother, I said, "Oh, Carolyn, look at this. Did you read this article on page 5?" I talked right over her. I hadn't really been listening to her.

Most of the time, what we call prayer is really us talking over God.

Too often when we pray, God is speaking, and we aren't listening. We're following our own agenda and talking over God. Prayer requires listening intently because God is talking. The sense of intimate awareness will be different for each of us, but in the moment of connection, we become aware that God is speaking, and we're hearing what God is saying.

I am unLearning the approach to prayer marked by one-way talking or reciting self-centered wish lists. I'm working to align my thoughts with God's thoughts and my actions with God's actions. Jesus really understood that prayer is about listening. Luke tells us that while Jesus was praying, heaven opened and he heard . the voice of God. (See Luke 3:21-22.)

When you really pray, you will be connecting with what God is saying. God spoke to the prophets long ago, and they faithfully recorded the teachings in the books we know as the Bible. But God didn't stop speaking once those writings were completed. Jesus told the early church, "I still have many things to say to you, but you cannot bear them now. When the Spirit of truth comes, he will guide you into all the truth; for he will not speak on his own, but will speak whatever he hears, and he will declare to you the things that are to come" (John 16:12-13). God wants to direct you into his future with a new word each day. It's essential to create God-listening moments in every day of our lives.

Danger lurks when I am not creating God-listening moments in my life to hear God's life-giving word for today. If I am not attuned to God's directions for my life and ministry, I fall into the trap of religion, hearing only yesterday's word, rather than the ongoing guidance of the living God, calling us to new and better things. Emerging church leaders live out of a deep awareness of the call of God.

New Christians demonstrate excitement and new life that comes from a fresh, dynamic relationship with Jesus. I always warn them, "Don't get religious." When they hang around religious people who don't have a fresh word from God, all they learn are rules and regulations, and quickly become like the critical, negative scribes of Jesus' day. UnLearning leaders have to constantly be listening for God's new word, or else risk feeding people with stale bread, stagnant prayers, and old advice. There is no life in that kind of religion.

God's Counsel Leads to Costly Action

We are committed to our children, and we are imperfect. We would give our lives for their success. How much more will God do, who wants to guide you and your congregation to the place of promise? God desires your success and the fulfillment of your created purpose. Radical prayer is boldly risking forward, trusting in God's guidance.

We often think of prayer as a complicated game of hide-and-seek, as if God is hiding from us and we are begging, "Come out, come out, wherever you are!" If you are a parent, do you go out and hide from your kids? If they are stumbling around, trying to find direction, do you hide and let them run into the wall? No. You give guidance and clear direction to your children.

When our daughter, Kristen, was in her senior year of college, she began applying to graduate schools. Her field of dietetics and nutrition is very competitive, so she was a little nervous. Being a dad, I did everything I knew to give her a competitive edge. I called her on the phone and told her to e-mail me her essays, offering to help her polish up her sound bites and make the essays sound better. I also advised her on how to handle interviews with aggressive confidence. As her dad, I wanted to make available to Kristen the collective wisdom that comes from my half-century of experience. We were on the phone for hours, and it was my dime, not hers.

If I as an imperfect parent—a broken person—desire to give all my wisdom and counsel to my children, how much more does God want to guide those who ask him for help? That's what radical prayer is about. God desires our best so much "that he gave his only Son" (John 3:16a) that you and I might succeed.

We are not going forward until we commit ourselves to radical prayer that compels us to risk forward in the counsel of God. It's not just about hearing God, but responding with radical action. The Bible says God is looking for people to speak to and bless—not because they're brilliant but because they are willing to do whatever God says. "Blessed rather are those who hear the word of God and obey it!" (Luke 11:28).

Imagine living in a desert climate where it doesn't rain even three inches a year, and God says, "Build a boat 450 feet long, 75 feet wide, and 45 feet high." The directive to Noah didn't make sense. How was Noah even going to find that much wood in the desert? Where would he acquire the financial backing, supplies, and workers that would be needed? But as a servant of God, Noah said, "It doesn't matter if it doesn't make sense, God. Here I am. Use me." (See Genesis 7:5.)

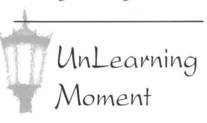

UnLearning Moment

Consider if you can sincerely pray this prayer: "Here I am, God. Everything I have is for your pleasure and your purpose. Amen."

The Matrix is a postmodern movie that uses a lot of biblical symbolism. Its physical fights compare to the spiritual fights with evil that we experience today. Neo is a man with a mission, and Morpheus is his godlike guide. The following dialogue begins as Neo, in his cubicle at work, answers a cell-phone call.

Morpheus:	Hello, Neo, do you know who this is?
Neo:	Morpheus?
Morpheus:	Yes, I've been looking for you, Neo. I don't know if you're ready to see what I want to show you, but unfortunately you and I have run out of time. They're coming for you, Neo . . .
Neo:	What . . . do they want from me?
Morpheus:	I don't know. But if you don't want to find out, you better get out of there.
Neo:	How?
Morpheus:	I can guide you out, but you must do exactly as I say.
Neo:	Okay.
Morpheus:	The cubicle across from you is empty. Go! Now!

Neo dashes across the small hallway and hides in an empty work area. His journey has many parallels to how God leads followers of Jesus. God tells us, "Listen to me. I can guide you, but you must do exactly as I say. Do it now."

God contacts us in unusual ways, and asks us to do things that may seem crazy. Neo trusted Morpheus at first, but soon becomes afraid when asked to do what seems impossible.

Morpheus:	When I tell you, go to the end of the row to the first office on the left. Stay as low as you can. Now. Good. Now there is a window. Open it.
Neo:	How do you know all this?
Morpheus:	The answer is coming, Neo. Outside, there is a scaffold. You can use it to get to the roof.
Neo:	No! It's too far away.
Morpheus:	There's a small ledge. It's a short climb. You can make it.
Neo:	No way. No way. This is crazy.
Morpheus:	Don't be controlled by your fear, Neo. There are

	only two ways out of this building. One is that scaffold. The other is in their custody. You take a chance either way. I leave it to you.
Neo:	This is insane! Why is this happening to me? What did I do?

Like Jesus' disciple Peter, who walked on water while he kept his eyes on Jesus, Neo took his eyes away from his source and looked down. Like God, Morpheus says he can't explain everything, but simply, "You've got to trust me." Walking with God does not always make sense and is not rational. Like Neo, we have two choices, two ways out: the radical, higher, costly way of finding the will of God and doing it, or going out in the custody of the forces of this world that lead to death.

One of Jesus' stories warns us to "be dressed for action and have your lamps lit; be like those who are waiting for their master to return from the wedding banquet, so that they may open the door for him as soon as he comes and knocks. . . . You also must be ready, for the Son of Man is coming at an unexpected hour" (Luke 12:35-36, 40).

UnLearning leaders know that God's call can come at any moment, and that we must be ready to follow the moving of the Spirit, wherever it may lead.

Leading into the Unknown

The currents of cultural change are so unpredictable that it's impossible to strategically plan five or ten years ahead. UnLearning leaders are prepared to follow Christ's voice fearlessly into a future of promise.

People often ask about my five- or ten-year plan for Ginghamsburg, but I don't have such a plan. If I were the one in charge, I'd have a plan. But I'm following Jesus. He is my life, and he has a vision for the future of our congregation. I don't know which way he will turn. I can only follow.

In 1994, while deep in prayer, I envisioned 10,000 people worshiping at Ginghamsburg by the year 2000. On-campus attendance has grown a lot since 1994, but it is still nowhere close to 10,000. We are reaching well over 10,000 people via the Internet, however, which wasn't even a possibility back in 1994! God saw what I could not see. Only by listening to God in prayer was I inspired to lead our congregation toward God's vision, though I had no idea how God would make it all happen.

I once overheard my friend Len Sweet call Ginghamsburg "the Velcro church." I asked what he meant, and he told me a story about when he brought a group of graduate students to our campus. They were touring our facility and walked past the prayer rooms on either side of the sanctuary. As they went by, students noticed a sign outside each room indicating whether the room was "in use" or "available." The sign is held on by Velcro. Examining how it worked, one student moved the sign from "available" to "in use," but it immediately fell to the floor. She picked it up and tried to reattach it, but it fell again. The same thing happened a third and a fourth time.

When the students returned to school, they discussed what they'd learned on their visit to Ginghamsburg. They observed that when the prayer sign was hung on the "in use" side, it would not stick because the Velcro had worn out. "Somebody there is praying," they concluded.

People who pray understand. When you are out on the edge, attempting the impossible, you can't help but live in an atmosphere of prayer. The life of an unLearning leader requires total dependence on God.

Look at the prayers of our Lord. As Jesus prayed the night before his death, he didn't say, "God, please make this as painless as possible." Instead, he prayed for God's will to be done, no matter what it cost him.

Radical prayer means listening for God's voice, seeking God's vision, and then devoting everything to living out that vision, no matter what it costs.

One Church That's UnLearning

Th3 Waters, Florence, Kentucky
www.th3waters.com

- **Quick Description:** An Experimental United Methodist Network of Organic Gatherings.
- **History:** Started in 2005 with a covenant between Florence United Methodist Church and the Kentucky Conference of the United Methodist Church.
- **Attendance:** 100 across 9 gatherings per week.

"Prayer has always been of great importance to Th3 Waters, but in a very simplistic, yet profoundly transformational way. The 'organic gatherings' meet each week, and rather than asking for prayer requests, we ask, 'What is up with your life?' We have found that this simple question is more effective when developing community with agnostics, Buddhists, and especially Christians than asking for prayer requests, which usually results in people telling you more about friends and loved ones than about themselves. As people share what is going on in their lives, the expectation is that everyone who is listening is asking themselves, 'How can we help?' or 'What are we going to do about it?' We immediately e-mail the 'what is up with our lives' to everyone else in the group and use this e-mail throughout the week as a prayer 'reminder.' We also have set alarms on our cell phones and work computers twice a day to remind us to stop whatever we are doing to pray for one another and those around us with the intention of slowly developing lives that are aware of God's presence. Our prayer is to be in constant relationship with God: a lifestyle of prayer and worship."

—D. G. Hollums, who with Florence UMC
planted this ancient/emerging-networked church; age: early thirties

7 Replicating the DNA

Leaders are the carriers of the congregation's DNA, spreading the word of God's vision for their community. This kind of leadership cannot be dictated, but rather will spread its influence by modeling the congregation's core values and mission, and empowering others to be part of the vision as well. The church is meant to be an organic movement, led by spiritual visionaries who mobilize lay-based ministry.

In first-century Israel, Nicodemus was the premier example of religious correctness. He practiced all the rules and regulations. The crowds recognized him as a religious authority.

But when Nicodemus met with Jesus, he heard some news that was difficult to accept. Jesus told him that he needed to be "born of the Spirit" (John 3:6). Nicodemus didn't understand, since he had already been born once, from his mother's womb. Jesus explained that in order to enter the kingdom of God, his very being would have to be invaded by the Spirit of God. His soul and character would have to become like those of Jesus, just as his physical birth ensured similarity and connectedness to his earthly parents.

Being infused with this "spiritual DNA" means complete immersion in Jesus. More than merely sampling the Christian life, immersion means taking on the nature, desires, passions, and behavior of Jesus. God creates new life in and through you.

I am unLearning the idea that Christianity is about believing in Jesus. It's really about the life of Jesus coming into your life and mine, forever transforming us into the likeness of our heavenly Father.

Spiritual leaders are the primary carriers of God's DNA in the church, those most attuned to God's intentions and visions for the congregation. They are the shapers of a church's vision and core values and the influencers of what the church embodies.

Christian leadership books today tend to deal with the ideology of leadership style, of embracing technology, or of innovative methodology. UnLearning leaders are going way beyond these emphases. They are interested in the spirit, content, and soul of leadership. They lead the church toward radical discipleship by replicating the DNA of the Holy Spirit throughout the church and community. Pastors work to develop the abilities and spiritual lives of other leaders in the congregation who will carry the DNA to the edges of the movement.

Mentoring Leaders As Trainer-Coaches

In the larger classes I took in college, the professor was the master teacher, while the graduate assistant was the accessible mentor who knew my name. The assistants were there to demonstrate and explain what the professor talked about. They converted ideas into action. They gave situation-specific feedback.

Discipleship emerges from a similar mentoring model. The apostles in the early church devoted themselves to prayer and the ministry of the Word. (See Acts 6:4.) They let others do everything else. Today the job of the spiritual leader remains the same: to lead the congregation in prayer and to teach the people the purposes and principles of God. He or she generally offers an overall prescription for the entire group, while trainer-coaches apply biblical life principles to the unique needs of each individual.

At Ginghamsburg, we say that celebration—our corporate worship of God—is important, but we also urge people to take their discipleship to the next level. By becoming part of a cell—a small group or class—they get to know people who will become their trainer-coaches in day-to-day life. Emerging churches have learned to empower as many as several thousand trainer-coaches to lead smaller worship communities or fellowship groups, and to focus on the personal development of each individual.

My primary responsibility in passing on the DNA of the Spirit to the people of Ginghamsburg Church is to be a leader to other leaders, a teacher to trainer-coaches. Through the breakdown of ministries for each age-group or special need, I can work with leaders specialized to those ministries, who recruit and train more leaders, so that each individual in the congregation has a mentor who knows them personally, thus personalizing spiritual guidance for them. These trainer-coaches each take responsibility for ten or so individuals in the congregation, sometimes meeting with them in small cell groups and sometimes one-on-one. A well-developed network of trainer-coaches can help us be faithful to our promises through demonstration, encouragement, and accountability, while transmitting the church's key ideas, values, and vision throughout the life of the entire congregation.

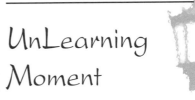

UnLearning Moment

What relationships can you think of in which you were or are a mentor to someone else or someone else has mentored you?

In very large congregations, this type of delegation is necessary, of course, but even in smaller congregations, the whole church can benefit from a leader who intentionally shares the vision and the responsibility for growing disciples. Trainer-coaches are at the heart of faith-building in the biblical plan, serving individuals and families in ways a pastor sometimes cannot, while maturing spiritually themselves as leaders of the congregation.

This isn't to say, of course, that senior leaders don't need people to help them grow spiritually. Every other Thursday morning at 6:45, I meet with three men on our church board. Together as leaders in this church, we hold one another accountable through the Word and prayer as we direct areas we're responsible for in the life of Ginghamsburg. This accountability group is essential to my spiritual well-being. Without it, I would be in no shape to lead others.

The Role of the Trainer-Coach

Erwin "Frosty" Brown is an American Legion baseball coach who has helped obtain some two hundred college scholarships for his players. Among those he has taken under his wing, ten young men have made it to the pros.

In our area of Ohio, anyone who wants to play college baseball works hard to make Frosty's Miami County team. Once players are on the team, Frosty becomes an integral part of their disciplined training, long before they play the first game of the season. He has a batting cage in his garage that "his boys" use throughout the year. His players can call him from anywhere and ask, "Coach, what's wrong with my swing?"

Frosty was my son Jonathan's summer coach for his final three years of high school. Many days I'd come home and see Jonathan talking with Frosty on the phone, receiving personal tips about his hitting or fielding. When it was time for Jonathan to head off to college, Frosty wrote a note to thank Jonathan for three years on the team. The letter also encouraged Jonathan in his upcoming years on an Ivy League university team. Frosty concluded his note by writing, "Never forget the old coach who believes in you."

Frosty replicates the DNA of the baseball world into each of his players with contagious passion and enthusiasm. And he continues to be a disciplined student of the game. Trainer-coaches in the life of the church must have contagious passion as well, and be committed to constant learning and discipline so they can pass wisdom on to those they mentor.

I coached Little League baseball for nine years while our children were growing up. It was a challenge to keep all fifteen players engaged, so we never had practice without an overall plan. We had to formulate a different plan for each child. For one home-run hitter, our goal was to lay the foundation for a possible future as a college player. For another boy on the team, the most important thing we could teach him was how to wear a baseball cap correctly so the other kids wouldn't tease him.

In the church setting, we need to help trainer-coaches break down the messages presented in each worship experience so they can formulate specific plans according to the needs of those in their cell groups. We design each weekend worship experience with supplemental curriculum for the trainer-coaches to use. It's also used in various small groups and by individuals in their daily devotional readings. We teach our trainer-coaches to regularly cover such areas of relationship-based discipleship as group-building skills, mentoring of others, prayer, service, financial stewardship, and witness. They take the people they're discipling through one or more of these elements, and then they give them the equivalent of homework.

It is the job of senior leadership to prepare the trainer-coaches to challenge every individual under their care to deepen his or her relationship with God and commitment to serve others. How that challenge is presented is different for each person, but discipline and resistance are key to helping anyone grow in faith.

After collapsing in a restaurant in August 2000, I realized I needed to take better care of my body, and began working with a personal trainer to increase my heart strength and my overall physical health. When we're doing weights, she always reminds me that strength comes only through resistance. When I think I can't do any more, she says, "Five more lifts." She wants me to push through the threshold of my resistance.

Resistance develops perseverance. Perseverance develops faith, and without faith, the fulfillment of God's promise will not happen. Much of the New Testament is a challenge to perseverance.

84

One example is Hebrews 10:23: "Let's keep a firm grip on the promises that keep us going" (The Message). Another translation calls us to "hold fast to the confession of our hope without wavering, for he who promised is faithful" (NRSV).

Paul likens our walk with Christ to athletic training. "Do you not know that in a race the runners all compete, but only one receives the prize? Run in such a way that you may win it. Athletes exercise self-control in all things; they do it to receive a perishable wreath, but we an imperishable one. So I do not run aimlessly, nor do I box as though beating the air; but I punish my body and enslave it, so that after proclaiming to others I myself should not be disqualified" (1 Corinthians 9:24-27).

Faith is hard work. One of the negatives of the modern church is that it has taught an easy believe-ism. We are saved by faith, not by belief. In the church today, many people think they're saved by right beliefs; but faith is different from belief. I believe a lot of things that don't impact my day-to-day living. I believe in exercise. I have no doubt that people live longer and are healthier if they exercise. Many of us believe in exercise, but believing is not the same as doing. Faith is acting on the directive of God.

The ultimate goal of trainer-coaches is to develop others into fully committed followers of Christ, capable of leading others and serving in a variety of capacities in the church and community.

Mobilizing Lay-Based Ministry

When it came to saving the world, God didn't send a professional minister. Jesus was not from the priestly tribe of Levi, but a carpenter's son from Nazareth. When Jesus spent all night in prayer deciding who should become his key leaders in changing the world (see Luke 6:12-13), he didn't choose professional clergy or religious leaders. He called fishermen and tax collectors. None of them could be confused with being professional ministers. The original church was a lay-based movement. The institutional church of today has lost momentum because of its emphasis on professional ministry.

Consider the difference in World War II between the Allied forces (including the United States) and the Axis forces (including Nazi Germany). The Allied focused on the platoon leader, who was on the front lines with a small group of about ten or so men. He was always moving toward the front, sold out to the mission. The Axis forces used a strategy of high command that made decisions far from the front line of the ordinary soldier, sometimes as far away as Berlin.

In the movie *Saving Private Ryan*, the character played by Tom Hanks isn't a professional soldier, but an English teacher, drafted for the cause of the mission. Yet you couldn't find a better platoon leader. He made the commitment that he wouldn't stop until he won the war. The Allied approach, represented in this character of the nonprofessional soldier who was able to understand and articulate the mission, is like the lay-based ministry that Jesus established for his church. Leaders need to be sold out to the cause. If they aren't inspired, they won't be inspiring. People can smell the passion of the Spirit. They need to be inspired as well as informed.

We learned in recent years that Ginghamsburg had too many administrative groups, and that not everyone leading those groups was adequately informed about the area of church life they were charged with overseeing.

Our area of Ohio is a hub of special-parts manufacturers for the automotive industry. As much as I love cars, though, I couldn't serve on one of their boards, even if my best friend chaired the board and personally tried to recruit me. A giant gap exists between someone who likes cars and someone who knows the business well enough to provide leadership counsel. In the church, any committed Christian is qualified to serve in some capacity, but if we want people who understand postmodern, emerging-church ministry, then we must get some of our brightest, sharpest, Spirit-filled leaders who are willing to make the investment to learn and become experts in our "business."

At Ginghamsburg, we reduced our administration to one board of nine people. We looked for three human resource specialists, three people with backgrounds in finance, and three people with business development expertise. All had to have the biblical qualities of elders. They, along with our seven-person staff executive team, are becoming informed together in the business of postmodern emerging church ministry. Each of these unpaid board members agreed to spend one week of their vacation each year attending a major national church training event together. This training enables the administrative function of the church to be a force-serving mission, rather than a group of control-seeking people.

I am unLearning solo ministry, and the attitude that clergy should behave like CEOs, hunting for the most qualified talent to work beneath them. Modern business practice falls far short of what spiritual leadership should be. Jesus intended his followers to be an organic movement of unpaid servants. Far from the model of power-hungry managers and paid staff, unLearning churches are led by chief spiritual visionaries who mobilize laypersons for ministry.

Our small groups structure at Ginghamsburg facilitates the replication of our DNA to all active laypeople in the congregation. Our paid and unpaid servants all emphasize the importance of Christ's command to serve others, and this core value is transmitted to every layperson at Ginghamsburg via the unpaid servants, the trainer-coaches who lead our small groups. Without having to be told, "Your small group should go serve the community," these people feel a driving passion to serve others in the name of Christ.

We tell the stories of what groups are doing through "Mission Moment" videos during worship, so others will know and similarly be inspired to serve. One video recently highlighted the work of one home group that became involved with a group of young teenage men in a foster home. Eager to reach out beyond itself, the group invited eight at-risk youths to come to

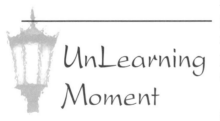

UnLearning Moment

What are you doing to help implant the DNA of your congregation's mission into each layperson?

church with them. They brought these young men to Ging-hamsburg for worship celebration and to The Avenue (our youth activities center) to play basketball. The group members felt enriched by the relationships they built with the young men, and the guys had such a great time they didn't want to go home! So they took their interaction a step further and offered to go to the young men's foster home to eat cookies and study the Bible together. The group experienced the joy of building trust through relationships, of speaking to the young men about Christ, and of leading them in a direction they weren't going before.

The video let everyone in worship that day experience the electricity of the group's connection with those young guys, and how the interaction made a difference for both the small-group members and the boys. "We did it as a one-time event, but it kept going," said one person from the home group. "My relationship with Christ has completely changed because of my experiences and times with these boys," said another. "They feel like family to us."

The video closed with the account of one of the young men's coming to faith in Christ. He concludes, "I never really cared about what happened in life, but now that I have a relationship with God, it's much easier to get along and not become mad so easily."

Think about the person who first connected you to Jesus Christ. Was it one of your parents? A friend? Whenever I take a show-of-hands poll, only a tiny group nominates a professional minister. The vast majority point to an unpaid servant such as a Sunday school teacher, youth leader, contagious neighbor, or coworker. The unpaid servants in your congregation will spread your congregational DNA and spell the success or failure of your mission.

Spreading the Fire

The people—both paid and unpaid—who make critical decisions for the direction of the church must be inspired, informed, empowered, and engaged. They need to breathe our church's strategy: to involve people in the life-transforming process of cell, celebration, and call. (I explain the theology behind this strategy in my book *Spiritual Entrepreneurs* (1995), and the practical application of it in *Out on the Edge* (1998), both published by Abingdon Press.) This breath—this spirit—carried by the leadership will become the spirit of the whole congregation.

I once asked our executive director to provide me with the financial giving statistics for our staff. It turned out that I was the top staff giver, and the next five were the others on our executive leadership team—the point leaders whom all the rest of the paid staff report to. Likewise, our nine board members were in the top 10 percent of givers across the entire church. You can go only as far as you're demonstrating to those who come after you.

I would rather have a church of twelve people who can replicate the DNA of the kingdom of God than a church of thousands that will infect people with something less. Choose leaders with the ability to influence and replicate the core vision and values of the movement of God. The kingdom of God is about Spirit, not size. If we're going to be the church at all, let's be the real thing, sharing the Spirit of the living God.

In ancient times, a fire carrier was the person responsible for moving the fire from one encampment to another as the tribe journeyed in its pursuit of food. This person often wore a specially made pouch that made it easier to transport a burning coal or ember.[1] For a nomadic tribe that depended on fire for cooking, warmth, or protection, the member who served as the fire carrier bore a huge responsibility for the tribe's survival.

You are a fire carrier of a different sort. You carry the fire of God's Spirit to places dependent on that flame of God-life in you, and work to spread that flame to empower other fire carriers. All who are faithful in Jesus have been "marked with the seal of the promised Holy Spirit" (Ephesians 1:13b). The fire of God is in them and goes wherever they go also. The job of the leader is to take those other fire carriers to the next place of God's leading. Our churches become what the leader embodies, and replicate the leader who shapes them.

One Church That's UnLearning

Spirit Garage, Minneapolis, Minnesota

www.spiritgarage.org

- **Quick Description:** Spirit Garage is a place to express your faith in a welcoming nonjudgmental setting with hot coffee and rock 'n' roll music.
- **History:** Evangelical Lutheran Church in America, started in 1997.
- **Attendance:** 115 in one Sunday-morning service.

"I am often unLearning and reLearning the importance of reminding, repeating, reiterating, and restating to our people again and again that our calling as a community is to be 'the church with the Really Big Door.' People get comfortable quickly and need to remember what made them comfortable here in the first place. Spirit Garage welcomes all makes and models—shiny and new, rusty and broken, but when people get comfortable they forget to go and do likewise, inviting others to drive in too. We like to say we do worship on the seashore, not in the temple. Our Mission is to offer the same grace given to us through Jesus, loving God and all people."

—Rob Norris-Weber, pastor, has been with the church
since fall 2004; age: early forties

8

Moving Together

UnLearning leaders have a gift for visioning what God can do. They paint a picture of a promising future for the congregation. To lead most effectively, they must partner with strategic managers, as Moses did with Aaron, so that everyone can lead from the sweet spot of their gifts, to honor God, benefit others, and experience personal fulfillment.

There are two kinds of people in the world: pioneers and settlers. Our area of Ohio used to be called the frontier. Many people left places like Philadelphia and Boston and set out for the West Coast. As they got going, they discovered that it was harder than they expected. People became sick. Wagon wheels broke. Oxen died.

They got as far as western Pennsylvania and started thinking that Pennsylvania looked rather appealing. All of a sudden these pioneers became settlers. They were paralyzed by the past memory of how good it was in Boston, where they had paved streets and streetlamps. Most of the pioneers never got past St. Louis.

It is tempting for us to settle for comfort over promise, and for easy over right. Leaders, however, continually look to the place of promise, as Moses did, and encourage people to continue the journey. Leaders see God's dream, and inspire others to see the same vision. Leaders don't put vision up for a vote, because they know people will always vote to go back to Egypt.

Egypt is all most of the Hebrew refugees ever knew. They brought so much baggage with them, so many pagan traditions, that when things got tough for them, they used all that baggage to build an incredible institutional edifice in God's name. All this effort turned out to be nothing more than a golden calf that looked like a god from the land they had just left behind.

Moses didn't know how to handle the people he was leading. He was focused on God's call and the vision of the Promised Land. The strongest voice Moses heard was the voice of God, and he would intentionally disconnect from people to go up on a mountain where he could more clearly hear God.

Aaron, on the other hand, did not lead others as much as he managed them. The strongest voice he heard was that of people around him, and he was very much in touch with their day-to-day struggles and complaints. On their own, neither Moses nor Aaron could have successfully led the Hebrews through the desert for forty years. Had either of them tried to be both a visionary and a manager, they likely would have failed. But together, Moses and Aaron formed a leadership team capable of guiding people toward the place God envisioned for them.

Leaders and Managers

During the summer of 1999, I was on the proverbial mountaintop, leading Ginghamsburg to our next place of promise. I looked back and saw grumbling. We had to say good-bye to some staff who were part of the difficulty. We lost two hundred people. For a while, I wondered if I was supposed to stay.

We discovered that leadership and management were moving at different paces. I learned that I'm good at vision but terrible at building the details to make the vision happen. I had to find someone who is ahead of me and recruit her to partner with us on staff. Enter Sue Nilson Kibbey, our Executive Pastor. I want to be included in the class of leaders who are willing for someone in the organization to be better than they are, and she is. She delights in strategic management, and builds the kinds of teams that help the priesthood of believers happen at Ginghamsburg.

My business card now says my role is Chief Dreamer. I have a near-identical card for more formal gatherings of pastors, but Chief Dreamer is an excellent description of my gift mix of prophetic teaching and evangelism. I love to proclaim God's vision for our world, as the Old Testament prophets did, and I am never fully happy so long as there's one more person out there who needs Jesus. But I can't live out these callings alone.

In addition to Sue and me, our executive team now consists of a Creative Director, a Director of Communications and Global Initiatives, a Teaching Pastor, a Director of Care and Counseling, a Chief Stewardship Officer, and a Facilities Manager. We're learning how to make leadership and management functions work together, and to use each person's unique gift mix for maximum impact in our congregation and community.

Working Your Sweet Spot

When you hit a tennis ball with the sweet spot of the racket, the ball takes off with seemingly little effort. The ball, almost on its own, just glides over the net. When the ball strikes outside that center area, you can still hit it over the net, but it's a lot harder. That awkward, vibrating feeling means you didn't connect in the sweet spot.

You and each person on your team have a sweet spot in which he or she is most effective and energetic in serving God's purpose. When you are living according to God's call in your life, feeling most deeply connected to God, and maximizing your personal potential, you're living in your sweet spot. UnLearning leaders know where their sweet spots are, and help others to find theirs as well. When every leader in your congregation is working in his or her sweet spot, there is no limit to what God can do through you.

94 People ask how I can keep the schedule I do, speaking at conferences across the U.S. and Canada, then coming back to preach at five worship celebrations each weekend at Ginghamsburg. The reason is that my sweet spot is in proclaiming the marvelous love of God in Jesus Christ. I may be physically tired, but my whole being is energized by the presence of God.

There's a world of difference between your "love to" and your "can do." For me, counseling comes from "can do" abilities. When I used to do counseling in ministry, I'd draw upon learning from my college degree in social work. I made myself spend an hour in preparation for the session, and then do twenty minutes of write-ups afterward. I can do counseling, but only with great energy drain.

UnLearning Moment

What is your sweet spot in ministry? Have you ever had to unLearn something you thought you were "supposed to" be good at? What tasks do you need to delegate in order to live more fully from your sweet spot?

I no longer do counseling ministry at Ginghamsburg. We found gifted laypeople in the church whose "love to" was pastoral ministry. Our crisis care ministry and counseling center have blossomed with paid professionals and unpaid servants doing pastoral care.

The apostles understood their sweet spots and said, in effect, "We cannot neglect the Word of God and prayer." They found people hard-wired by the Spirit who capably and passionately did food distribution for the widows in the community. God received honor, the whole community of faith benefited, and everyone operating out of their sweet spots experienced joy. "The word of God continued to spread; the number of the disciples increased greatly in Jerusalem, and a great many of the priests became obedient to the faith." (See Acts 6:1-7.)

We must unLearn habits that keep us from connecting with our sweet spots, things we feel we're "supposed" to be good at that really prevent us from living in the center of our passion and giftedness. Leaders can't live out of the "can do" long-term and be healthy at the same time. Sometimes, we can't avoid these activities, but the wise leader will strategize how to move more into the "love to."

How can you discern whether you're living out of "love to"? If you're living in your sweet spot, you can't help but honor and glorify God. It will benefit and bless other people. It will bring you joy. Everything you touch will be multiplied for God's purpose.

Ask those who know you well—work colleagues, people you're mentoring, and your spouse. Ask them to describe what you seem to be most motivated to do (your heart passion) and where you are most fruitful (your effectiveness). If you really want to be gutsy, ask your children what your ultimate passion is. They can identify it in a moment, and tell you if your passion is your work, your hobby, your lifestyle, or even if it is God.

That passion is where great work will be done.

Life Outside the Sweet Spot

As we grow older, we have a tendency to decelerate in our life dreams. Sometimes self-doubt hits us. Physical energy and stamina wane. Years of coming against negative and resistant people begin to take their toll. We begin to wonder if we still have what it takes. Instead of being a source of healing and life to other people, we can become a source of irritation, confusion, and conflict. Once a young dreamer, we soon become an aging cynic. We begin to compromise and produce a life that is successful but not satisfying, trading our mission for materialism.

Burnout and even sin result when we choose to live outside our sweet spots, giving energy and passion to things that are only of earthly significance. We pour ourselves into our families, our jobs, our churches, or our hobbies, all to the neglect of God, underestimating the purpose for which God sent us and living instead for our own purposes. When I am not working from my sweet spot,

I will be more prone to anger, quarrels, dissension, strife, idolatry, lust, and jealousy. By elevating my own self-importance, I lose my receptiveness to God's daily re-creation of my heart.

According to Ephesians, God is constantly poised "to accomplish abundantly far more than all we can ask or imagine" (3:20b) according to the Spirit working in us. But when we are simply trying to serve our own purposes, our own voices replace the voice of God. This is the very root of sin, making us ego-centered people, the center of our own universe and oblivious to others' needs and feelings.

Jesus said, "If any want to become my followers, let them deny themselves and take up their cross and follow me. For those who want to save their life will lose it, and those who lose their life for my sake will find it" (Matthew 16:24-25). As the church, the community of Christ's followers today, we must deny ourselves and live for the mission to which we were called and specially equipped.

Drucker's Three Questions

Each paid and unpaid servant in your congregation has a particular gift mix—a particular sweet spot out of which he or she must work. The key to effective church leadership is in helping those uniquely gifted people work together in an arrangement and environment that has maximum impact for overall mission.

Leadership and management expert Peter Drucker often asked people, including church leaders, to consider three questions when trying to unify a team around a particular vision.[1]

1. What Is Our Business?

The church's business is life transformation. It's not programs. It's not church-growth numbers. It's not to build brick-and-mortar edifices. The ultimate goal is to bring people to Jesus. Church programs won't change anybody, but people will grow in the context of a vital community.

The Gospel account of Jesus healing a paralytic (see Mark 2:1-12) demonstrates that the man's four friends clearly understood the goal of the business. "When they could not bring him to Jesus because of the crowd, they removed the roof above him; and after having dug through it, they let down the mat on which the paralytic lay" (Mark 2:4). They had to tear down the existing structure to get their friend to Jesus. Structures have to give way to mission.

2. Who Is Our Customer?

God loves and desires a relationship with each and every human being. Therefore, everyone is the church's "customer," in that we are called to show God's love to every person. Some churches specialize in ministering to certain demographic groups, tailoring their worship services and fellowship offerings to the felt needs of particular segments of the population. For example, at Ginghamsburg, we emphasize building the next generation. We make a point of targeting twenty-five- to forty-five-year-old people who have children at home. They have been turned off by the established church and are interested in pursuing radical faith. This doesn't mean people without children and people older than forty-five (which I have been for a while now!) have no place in our congregation, but that we all are working toward the goal of sowing seeds of faith that will live on in future generations.

Whatever local demographics each congregation emphasizes, however, Christ does specify some populations to whom all Christ-followers are to show extra consideration. Jesus says, "I was hungry and you gave me food, I was thirsty and you gave me something to drink, I was a stranger and you welcomed me, I was naked and you gave me clothing, I was sick and you took care of me, I was in prison and you visited me" (Matthew 25:35-36). We are especially called to serve the hungry, the thirsty, the alienated, the naked, the sick, and the imprisoned. The church does not exist to simply sustain itself, but rather to reach out to the poor and marginalized. No matter what programs we plan or experiences we offer for the people who show up to worship each weekend, we must remember that our true purpose is not to bring the world into the church, but to take the church into the world.

3. What Does the Customer Consider to Be of Value?

The answer to this question varies from church to church, as each seeks to serve its own community first and foremost. According to a major survey in our area of Ohio, people value (a) personal life management as it relates to stress, (b) parenting skills and help with their children, and (c) healthy marriage development.

It is no accident that McDonald's builds playgrounds on the front of their buildings. They understand the felt needs of their customers. Do we?

The vision that unLearning leaders cast for their congregations depends on the needs that God wants the church to meet in each community and across the globe. Cultivating the talents of key leaders in the congregation and assembling a team that complements one another's skill sets means keeping these needs in mind as everyone works together to transform lives for Christ.

One Church That's UnLearning

Coast Hills Community Church
www.coasthillschurch.org

- **Quick Description:** A church helping every follower of Christ discover and respond to God's calling on his or her life.
- **History:** Nondenominational, started in 1985.
- **Attendance:** 2,800 in three services.

"I'm unLearning that people need to see their pastor as having it 'all together.' It seems the older generations don't really want to know that their leaders have feet of clay, but the younger generations know they do—and they want to hear them admit it. When we share our pain in the context of a sermon or lesson, and when we take off our own masks and let people inside, it endears them to us as well as increases our credibility. Transparency and authenticity are extremely valuable in communicating the grace and love of Jesus Christ. None of us can make it alone. I think the younger generations realize this more than ever and are willing to take off the facade of rugged individualism and reach out to others for community."

—Ken Baugh, senior pastor since 2004; age: early forties

9 A Higher Value

As leader and chief visionary of your congregation, one of the most important things you can do is keep your focus on God. In a world of countless distractions, increasing value placed on speed and convenience, and cheapening of true divine encounters, help those you lead pursue the better, higher standard of fulfillment that Jesus proclaims.

I was born toward the end of the Industrial Age, which lasted almost three hundred years. We're now in the Information Age. When this country was founded, decades would pass before the available knowledge doubled. Today, information doubles approximately every eighteen months, and the rate continues to accelerate.

Whether we like it or not, if we're going to survive and compete in the twenty-first century, we must deal with today's commodities of value: speed and information. Everything in today's culture says they are the must-have essentials for success, and that you can't survive without them. Technology has certainly made life more convenient in some ways, but it has also blurred the line between work and play, between work time and personal time.

I was in a movie theater with my wife and was distracted by cell phones ringing during the show. Listening in, I couldn't help noticing that people were doing business during the movie. "You've got to close that deal by Wednesday," a man near me was saying. People in today's high-technology culture have lost the ability to separate business and leisure. I've seen people on their BlackBerry devices at restaurants and even in church. Their quest for success and wealth creates not only an infatuation with but a complete dependence on speed and information. They lose perspective on what this life is really about.

Beyond "the Scratch"

My friend Wayne Cordeiro, a church leader in Hawaii, has a vivid illustration he uses to demonstrate the foolishness of limiting ourselves to an earthly perspective. In his book *Doing Church as a Team*, he says to imagine a cable stretched out in front of you that extends in both directions farther than the eye can see. The cable represents the continuum of time that goes into eternity.

> *To contrast the brevity of our earthly existence with that of eternity, I would take out my ballpoint pen and draw a vertical scratch on the extended cable. Then I would tell you that the width of that scratch mark (about 1/32 of an inch) represents how long our life on earth is in comparison with all eternity. Not very long!*
>
> *But do you know what most people do? They not only live on that scratch, but they also love that scratch. They kiss the scratch. They save for that scratch. They hoard for that scratch. They live scratch lives, have scratch businesses, and have scratch families with scratch hopes and scratch dreams.*
>
> *But God so loved that scratch that He sent His only begotten Son to die for those who live there. Yet many still don't know about this gift called eternal life! They're still hanging on to the scratch. They try to elongate it, stretch it and extend it as much as possible. But even in the midst of their attempts, they know deep inside that there's got to be something more.[1]*

Yet we continue to focus on the scratch. We have little-scratch dreams, drive little-scratch cars, live in little-scratch homes, and raise little-scratch children. When we die, we leave behind little-scratch accomplishments.

A friend of mine told me that he needed a boat. "I've worked hard all my life, and I deserve it," he said. "I need something that will help me get away from it all."

He took the boat out twice last year and made twelve payments. Talk about diminishing returns! You end up serving whatever kingdom you buy into.

What is the lure of these kingdoms? Each is an enticement to pleasure, prestige, or possessions. When Jesus went out into the wilderness, Satan tempted him by offering him the whole world, and all its kingdoms. (See Matthew 4:1-11.) "All these I will give you, if you will fall down and worship me."

There's the catch.

Life isn't about personal gain and pleasure. It's about pleasing God. Jesus resisted Satan's temptation, saying, "Away with you, Satan! For it is written, 'Worship the Lord your God, and serve only him.'"

Even though Jesus had a heavenly Father of great wealth, he became poor so that through his poverty, you and I would be rich. What a God! The Son of God left infinity and came to this finite planet. Through his poverty, you and I discover true wealth.

This wealth isn't only for intelligent or rich people. It's for all people.

This wealth can't be measured through beauty or material prosperity.

This wealth is about transformation. Jesus' wealth is about new life in him.

When we die, God is not going to ask how much money we made, how big our organization was, or how talented and successful we were in sports or other hobbies. The number one question God is going to ask you and me is "What have you done with my Son, Jesus Christ, and the incredible gift of life?"

Possessions do not give life. You buy a bigger house, which means you have bigger payments, which means you work longer hours, which means you end up spending more time away from your

104 family. Possessions tend to bite us back many times, and they rob us of life. Advertisers forget to tell us about that hidden price tag.

Sometimes I find myself checking out the worship bulletin and becoming discouraged if the attendance report says we're down from last week. I am unLearning the CEO leadership model that obsesses over numbers and figures, becoming distant from the people of the congregation, clouded by a sense of superiority and entitlement. Life can't be found in that definition of success. My hope is in Jesus, who always points us to a higher standard of success.

There is a real danger in the pastor-as-CEO outlook, because it carries an expectation of a comfortable lifestyle, rather than living as a servant to God and God's people. There is a consumer mentality that permeates American culture, and even the church of Jesus Christ has been deeply infected by it. This consumer mentality is the antithesis of the kingdom of God. God's call to the church and its leaders is to live a life of servanthood, not a life of greed and entitlement.

UnLearning Moment

What views about the church do you need to unLearn in order to adopt God's standard for measuring success?

The Temptations of Leadership

King David provides the perfect example of a leader whose call and passion for praising and serving the Lord was derailed by the temptation to embrace the values of the world and of his kingly status. David was a Spirit-appointed leader, chosen by God even as a boy to become the leader of Israel.

God interwove David's boyhood life experience and skills with a greater spiritual purpose in mind. When the prophet Samuel looked for the person to anoint as the next king, God guided him to look beyond outward appearance. David was clearly not the logical choice. His brothers were all older, and apparently bigger, stronger, better-looking, smarter, and more skilled. David was just a child. The Lord explained to Samuel, concerning one of the older brothers, "Do not look on his appearance or on the height of his stature, because I have rejected him; for the LORD does not see as mortals see; they look on the outward appearance, but the LORD looks on the heart" (1 Samuel 16:7).

God selected David based on his heart, for David had a passionate faith, an incredible affair of the heart with God. God even affirmed David as "a man after his own heart" (1 Samuel 13:14b). David had a God-given passion for significance, for making a difference, and he led Israel into a golden age of enlarged borders, power, and influence. In situation after situation, he followed God's leading. He was successful as a leader, and the temptation toward entitlement came subtly.

Didn't he deserve to stay home once in a while? Hadn't he trained enough soldiers to fight in his place? Wasn't living comfortably an appropriate next phase in his life as leader? David felt he was so privileged that he didn't need to go into battle. He delegated that task, and his decision compromised his spirit. He forgot that, first and foremost, he was the spiritual leader to his people. "In the spring of the year, the time when kings go out to battle . . . David remained at Jerusalem" (2 Samuel 11:1). He saw a beautiful woman named Bathsheba bathing on her rooftop, and despite the fact that he was told she was someone else's wife, "David sent messengers to get her, and she came to him, and he lay with her" (2 Samuel 11:4a). He compounded this first abuse of power with another, arranging for Bathsheba's husband to be murdered when they discovered she was pregnant. (See 2 Samuel 11:14-25.)

David let the power that came with his leadership become a roadblock to the calling he had long felt to serve God in his capacity as king. The passion he had felt for God was quickly forgotten when temptation presented itself.

Keeping God in Sight

How often do we lose sight of God when the going gets tough? Or even simply after some period of time has passed since our last profound experience of God? Chances are, we felt our call to

Christian leadership in the context of a life-changing experience when we truly felt the presence and heard the voice of God. The energy and excitement we feel in the aftermath of such experiences motivates us for ministry, but that feeling cannot last forever, and we must be able to stay faithful to God and our call to provide true spiritual leadership to our congregations and those on our team.

A group of youth and adult leaders from our church went to Mexico on a mission trip and had an eye-opening encounter. They came back saying, "We've seen the Lord!" People who have reality-changing Jesus-recognition experiences can't wait to tell other people about them. But these kinds of experiences are few and far between, and they have a tendency to fade quickly.

Some people gauge their spiritual health based on the recentness and frequency of their "mountaintop experiences," these spiritual highs where God seems so close. The top of the mountain, however, is never the final destination. When you reach the top, you're only halfway there. When you go skiing, you go to the top so that you can come back down. It's the same with our spiritual lives.

As quarterback for the Dallas Cowboys, Troy Aikman led his team to a Super Bowl victory. Instead of celebrating the night away with his team, however, he sat in his room, drank a beer by himself, and felt an overwhelming sense of depression. During his early teenage years, he had thought all his problems would be solved the moment he turned sixteen and was able to buy a car. They weren't. So he looked for a higher mountain to climb. His ambition became to play pro football. The Super Bowl win took him to the top of pro football, and yet he still found himself asking, "Now what?" He didn't know how to live on the descent or in the valleys of life.[2]

When people climb Mount Everest, few fatalities occur on the way up. More climbers actually die on the way down the mountain. When they reach the summit, they are so awed by the view and their accomplishment that they forget it is not the final destination. They still need to make it safely back down. They spend too much time at the top, using up their precious resources, and don't have the energy to make it all the way back down.

To fully encounter God, we can't stay at the top. Many followers of Jesus have had powerful experiences with God. The cloud of God's presence comes over us. We have a sense of awe and wonder. We realize that we're in the presence of the living Lord, and yet hours later we find ourselves in the low place of self-doubt and confusion. The truth, however, is that while we hear God on the mountain, we see God when we come down and serve people.

Jesus had a mountaintop meeting with God that was truly awe-inspiring, not just for him, but for Peter, James, and John, who were with him. The scripture says that "he was transfigured before them, and his face shone like the sun, and his clothes became dazzling white" (Matthew 17:2). The disciples wanted to build tents so they could stay on the mountaintop, but Jesus told them to get up, and they descended the mountain together. Jesus modeled that any real God-encounter will lead us to get down and work where people are.

People in our churches are sometimes like the disciples, wanting to stay on the mountaintop, wanting more spiritual food. Some people at Ginghamsburg say, "Mike, you don't feed me anymore." Many of these people forget that our connection with God is never complete until we make the commitment to sacrifice our personal needs and come down from the mountains of our personal spiritual journeys to serve the needs of the oppressed and hurting all around us.

Building Our Spiritual "Muscle"

Spiritual hunger can appear in many different forms. We don't always recognize it as spiritual in nature. It can appear as restlessness, longing, dissatisfaction, and even boredom. Things that offer immediate gratification do not ultimately fill us up. When we're bored we eat, shop, buy a new car, or otherwise engage our consumer mentality. Or we may find a little project to become involved with, never realizing that the hunger pangs rumble from a deeper place in our beings. Consumer binges or comfort foods can never satisfy this hunger. God alone is the bread of life.

By emphasizing spiritual formation as a lifelong discipline, unLearning leaders can empower their congregations to take responsibility for their own "feedings," building up their spiritual strength with sustained practices. It is not enough to have a deeply moving retreat weekend and then let the Bible grow dusty for weeks on end. Spiritual muscles are like physical muscles. When we don't use them, they atrophy. They deteriorate.

I learned that lesson the hard way one year when my son and

UnLearning Moment

How is your relationship with God right now? What disciplines do you need to work on to be in better "shape" as a follower of God and as a spiritual leader for others?

I went skiing in the Rockies. We had been going to West Virginia to ski for years, but then Jonathan latched on to the idea of skiing in the Rockies. I told him that when his basketball season was over, we'd go ski out west together. I would always pull out the stairclimber for a couple weeks before we went to West Virginia, and I started working out four weeks ahead of time to prepare for skiing in the high elevation and steep slopes of the Rockies.

One morning we were eating breakfast at home in Ohio, elevation 800 feet, and the next day we were in the Rockies at 11,000 feet. Jonathan, who had just finished four months of basketball, increasing his lung capacity and leg strength, wanted to ski from the very top of the mountain, above the tree line, at 13,000 feet. At the end of the lift, we had to hike up to the top, where they never groom the snow. The mountain was covered with two feet of fresh powder. I was over my knees in powder skiing down, and when you ski in powder, you have to jump. I got down to the tree line and was wiped out! I needed oxygen. When you're forty-something, you can't expect to get prepared to ski in the Rockies in just four weeks.

The same is true in our walk with God. Most of us have neglected our spirits. UnLearning leaders go beyond the latest leadership fads and technological innovations to the ancient practice of spiritual formation—the practice of daily disciplines that Jesus was committed to, such as prayer, solitude, meditation on the Scriptures, fasting, fellowship, service, generous giving, and commitment to simplicity of lifestyle.

Think of the fairy tale *Snow White and the Seven Dwarfs*. It's the story of a beautiful young woman who ate a poisoned apple and fell into a deep sleep. No one could awaken her, not even her seven vertically challenged friends! That is what we are like when we neglect our spirits. The reality of our being goes into hibernation, and no one can revive us.

In the story, a prince came along and awoke Snow White with a kiss, and she instantly knew that this was the one she'd been created for. This is what Jesus Christ does in our lives. Do you remember what it felt like the first time you were awakened by Jesus Christ? The manger scene we pull out every Christmas reminds us that while we were sleeping, God kissed us. God loved us and created a plan for us. God wants to restore the broken relationship and bring us back to life.

It's not enough just to be awakened, however. We've got to decide to follow. Human beings know what we should do. We know what we're supposed to do. We must get up and act on what we know to be true. How many people have been awakened in their relationship with God but still haven't climbed out of bed? Jesus has come and made this incredible announcement that God loves everyone and has a plan for each life, but too many people never really get started. Your role as leader is to help them take that step toward a lifetime of active faith.

One Church That's UnLearning

New Life Fellowship, Queens, New York City
www.newlifefellowship.org and
www.emotionallyhealthy.org

- **Quick Description:** We exist to glorify God by leading people to a personal relationship with Jesus and by demonstrating the love of Christ across racial, cultural, economic, and gender barriers.
- **History:** Started 1987 with 3 people.
- **Attendance:** 1,100 people from over 65 nations.

"I am unLearning serving God out of duty and learning to serve him out of joy and delight. During the first seven years of pastoring, we were growing, planting congregations, and adding people to God's kingdom. The bad news was that my heart for God and people was slowly shrinking. More important, my wife, the one person to whom I had vowed to love well the rest of my life, felt unvalued. She felt like a single mom. I was too busy and overloaded to have energy for her and our children. My focus was on results, effectiveness, and growth. Through sheer grace from God, I began to see that I was saving the whole world and losing my own soul (Matthew 16:26).

"A gradual but dramatic personal transformation followed in my personal life, marriage, and family. I then led the church through the same journey, a journey we now call emotionally healthy spirituality. I firmly believe that God's greatest call for us as leaders is to love him, ourselves, and others well. Paul argues that that is the criteria for success. This path to emotional health has been painful and required a great deal of unLearning. The joy and fruit, however, have been inestimable!"

—Pete Scazzero, lead pastor, has been with the church from the start; age: early fifties. He is the author of *Emotionally Healthy Spirituality* (Nelson, 2007) and *Emotionally Healthy Church* (Zondervan, 2003).

A Theology of Sweat

Outreach goes way beyond bringing somebody to church. UnLearning leaders demonstrate the kingdom of God on earth, showing people what human relationships can look like when Jesus Christ is Lord. UnLearning leaders will do all they can, give all they can, and serve all they can until everyone gets to the table of God.

One mistake church leaders make is thinking that their success and worth as a pastor are in doing it "by the book," adhering strictly to the rule book of their denomination or by legalistically focusing on every detail in *the* Book—the Bible itself.

Jesus lived in an era when well-trained religious leaders were on every corner, but these leaders were neither relevant nor contagious. They knew all 613 commandments in the Torah, and were quick to correct people if they didn't follow them precisely; but the people were not looking for correction, they were seeking the presence of God. Some left the comforts of Jerusalem's magnificent temple, letting their search for God take them out into the wilderness to listen to a prophet named John who wasn't deemed religiously correct or within the boundaries of traditional expressions of faith.

John was different from the religious leaders of his day because of what his life displayed. He lived simply, clothed in camel's hair and eating locusts and honey. John was someone who knew and experienced God in a way that seemed authentic, and people were drawn to that.

John Wesley, the eighteenth-century evangelist and founder of Methodism, was an innovator, taking the church to the people by preaching along the roadsides of rural England. He was reprimanded by the Anglican establishment for this, but the movement of circuit-riding preachers he sparked spread the gospel to people far outside the traditional church. One biographer of Wesley described him as "a flame going up and down the land, lighting candles such as, by God's grace, would never be put out."[1]

Catch on fire for God, and people will come to watch you burn.

UnLearning leaders know what it's like to feel the burn. I am unLearning the idea that my primary objective as a leader is to grow, innovate, compete, or inform. Instead, spiritual leaders are called to be a visual demonstration of God's power and presence on earth.

UnLearning Moment

What is one way you have led your congregation to go against popular religious culture to truly demonstrate the love of Jesus?

Living the Presence of God

Jesus spoke extensively about the kingdom of God. The Gospels contain more than one hundred references to God's kingdom. Jesus emphasized that the power of God's kingdom has come to earth. Through Jesus, it was already present among his followers.

Jesus taught as one with authority, with power that fully demonstrated a holy confidence that might be summarized as, "Watch me and see that the presence of God has appeared." The Bible says that "the crowds were astounded at his teaching" (Matthew 7:28b) because it was different from what the scribes and Pharisees modeled as they taught.

Today, the world is not interested in Christianity because we aren't known as people who live what we say. On the other hand, Buddhism is one of the fastest growing religions in America because its followers tend to practice what they believe. Buddhism is a religion centered in practice rather than in doctrine. Un-Learning leaders are returning to the ancient Christian emphasis on practice and faith development rather than a narrow view of information-transfer.

Too many Christians reduce faith to easy "beliefism," as if they had a Monopoly-like card reading, "You are authorized to pass Go and skip hell because you have made the correct mental decision." Others commit themselves to social activism without a real commitment to the ultimate servant whom they are to emulate. A Christian is not someone who makes an intellectual statement of belief, or who commits to a lifestyle of little do-good-isms that have no spiritual motivation. A Christian is someone who is like Jesus.

In its earliest years, the word *Christian* was derogatory. It meant "Christ-people," or "little Christ," and while such a comparison was a badge of honor for Christ's followers, Roman soldiers didn't see anything honorable about the Christlike lifestyle, and would mock Christians for their peacefulness and generosity.[2]

Roman armies had an inexpensive way of outfitting their troops for the winter. Soldiers could stop anyone and say, "I'm a soldier; give me your coat," and you had to do it. They had a similar way of moving equipment. A soldier could stop anyone and command, "Carry my pack," and you had to carry it for one mile. At the end of the mile, you could stop, set it down, and say, "I've done my duty according to Roman law." The soldier would then grab another person.

"Not these Christians!" said the Romans. "When we take one of their coats, they voluntarily offer more: 'Would you like the shirt I bought to match it?' Or at the end of a mile, they say 'I'm ready to go a second mile.' "[3]

It has been said that the greatest distance in the universe is the gap between *knowing* what's right and *doing* what's right. I regularly speak at conferences, and somewhere in my talk, I usually mention how Ginghamsburg makes membership a serious commitment, so, unlike other churches whose weekly attendance is lower than the number of people on their membership rolls, we have about 5,000 in worship each weekend, but only 1,300 who have made the commitment to membership. I include time for questions during or after my message, and one question has stuck with me for a long time: "You have thousands of people in attendance each week, but only a third of them are committed enough to join? How many of your attendees are really committed to the Christian life, then?"

I responded that out of the seven to eight thousand people who show up on our campus in a given month, I would hope that there were five hundred people who were living the Christian life, daily acting on the decision they've made to follow Jesus and sacrificially serve his mission in the world.

A lot of people have made decisions for Jesus. Very few have ever acted on those decisions. It is so much harder to live the gospel than it is to simply believe. That is why, more than ever, leaders must model what life is like when Jesus is Lord.

Being Christ in the World

Eight hundred years before Christ was born, the prophet Isaiah wrote the prophecy we now see on countless Christmas cards and hear sung in Handel's *Messiah*: "A virgin shall conceive, and bear a son, and shall call his name Immanuel" (Isaiah 7:14b KJV). Immanuel means "God with us."

The miracle of Christmas is that God was born in human form.

The miracle of the Christian life is that God is born *in us*.

Christianity is not fundamentally a belief system. It is not an academic proposition to be defended. God has supernaturally entered the life of all who give themselves to Jesus Christ, and that life begins to grow in us. As Jesus lives through us, we are God-bearers. We are marked by the life of God. We carry the light of Christ. The church is most effective when its leaders demonstrate God's light and life to others. We are God's hands and feet in the world.

Our mission is the continuation of Jesus' mission to a suffering world. Jesus said, "The one who believes in me will also do the works that I do and, in fact, will do greater works than these" (John 14:12). Don't underestimate the implications of these words! This promise opens new windows onto our life missions. Doing "greater works" than even Jesus did gives us the assurance that when we leave planet Earth, the Holy Spirit will have conceived and given birth to God's purpose through our life energies.

Postmodern people are looking for authenticity. They do not seek explanations about God so much as they seek authentic life-demonstration of biblical relevance. UnLearning leaders are more about a demonstration of a greater-works-than-these, authentic faith than about simplistic Jesus slogans and magic faith formulas. Their greatest persuasion point is authentic life experience, not argumentative reasoning.

In an encounter Jesus had with his disciple Peter after the Resurrection, he asked Peter the same thing three times: "Do you love me?" (see John 21:15-17). Each time, Peter said, "Yes," and each time Jesus told him how to live that love: "Then feed my sheep."

Jesus' preoccupation is with people who are in need. He is not concerned about our claims to love and serve him, but our willingness to demonstrate that love through caring for those who are still on the outside and not yet experiencing God's party. "If you love me," he is saying, "you will be my connection to those who are not here."

Jesus is saying that if you want to experience God, you have to be serving people. UnLearning churches personally demonstrate the kind of authentic faith that embodies involvement with the lost and oppressed.

Don't Eat 'Til Everyone's at the Table

One of the images Jesus often used for the community of God's people was that of a dinner party. In several places, the New Testament writers describe a fantastic party, a banquet to end all banquets, put on by God. Anyone knows that if you are going to a dinner party, you need to be aware of certain principles of etiquette. And what was the first rule of table manners your mother taught you? Don't eat until everyone is at the table.

The night before our daughter, Kristen, was graduated from college, our son, Jonathan, had an important baseball game. So, Carolyn went on to be with Kristen while I attended the game and then drove with Jonathan through the night to get to Kristen's graduation. We arrived at 3:00 a.m. and crashed into bed. When we got up, we didn't have time for breakfast because we had to get to the graduation early enough to find prime seats for taking pictures. After the graduation, we congratulated Kristen's friends and then moved Kristen out of her apartment. By the time we finished, it was late afternoon and we still hadn't eaten. I was bordering on famished. We had invited sixteen family members and friends who were making the journey to the graduation out for a celebratory dinner. We drove to the restaurant and had to wait for all sixteen people to get there. The food finally started coming, but not everyone's came at the same time. Mine came out first, so I cheated a little on my etiquette. When no one was looking, I'd grab a little piece of my food and put it in my mouth.

Do we as Jesus' party guests do the same thing? We've learned that it's rude to eat before everyone is seated and served, but when we come to this wonderful spiritual banquet of God, we start scrambling for the best seats. We fight for the best parking spots. We crowd ahead of others in the coffee line. We cry out, "Feed me!" rather than focusing on what God is focused on: gathering all those who aren't yet at the table.

The biblical story, from Genesis to Revelation, describes God's relentless pursuit of those who are lost. Besides Jesus' question to Peter, the only other place where Jesus repeats the same point three times in a row is in Luke 15. He tells three parables about lost things, all with the same point: lost people matter to God.

"Which one of you, having a hundred sheep and losing one of them, does not leave the ninety-nine in the wilderness and go after the one that is lost until he finds it?" asks Jesus (Luke 15:4). Does your heart feel complete when ninety-nine are in the house, or have you saved energy, effort, a good seat, and the best parking space for the one who's still on the outside?

We have some close relatives who are precious people but who make it to church only about twice a year. Every time Ginghamsburg's leadership team sits down to prayerfully plan worship, I think, "Is this something that would be appetizing to them?" I also think about all the kids I've coached in baseball through the years: "Will what we're doing connect with them?" I don't want to eat until everyone is at God's table.

UnLearning Moment

Who do you know and care about that is not yet a regular guest at God's table? What can you do to help this person connect with God?

Don't Pull the Chair Out from under People

The first time I got spanked in school (back when that was accepted practice in schools), I was in fourth grade, and I had pulled the chair out from under a classmate. I learned the hard way that you just don't do that. The same is true in church.

Sometimes, once we've invited someone to join us at the table, we metaphorically pull the chair right out from under them, not practicing the love we promised them. Sometimes our manner communicates, "I love you, but until you get your act together, you are sort of a second-class citizen. I will tolerate you, but you are really a source of disappointment." We welcome with our words, but we belittle with our actions and church structures. Jesus welcomed all people to dine with him, and he was willing to eat even with people the religious authorities considered unclean. God welcomes us, and we need to remember that it's certainly not because we're worthy.

Jesus' parable of the prodigal son (see Luke 15:11-32) is essentially about a teen who grows up in a God-centered home with all the graces for life and success. His family can't believe that he's their son when he announces at Christmas break that he's not going back to college for his second semester. "I need to find myself, and live a little," he says. He decides to travel through Europe for a few months, and he spends all his college money on the wrong kinds of things. He begins to experiment with things that soon become addictions. His infrequent prayers are really worries about the possibilities of contracting a sexually transmitted disease. Things get worse and worse, and he comes to a point where he doesn't even know how to get back home. Yet, as someone created for relationship, he longs for his father's love.

Here's the point of Jesus' story: long before the young man gets his act together, and while he is still a long way off from where he needs to be, the father goes running toward him. Not only does he pursue his son, but when he finds him, he quickly forgives and embraces him. The father is willing to get his son's stench on his own clothes!

I am a part of the church of Jesus Christ because when I was a teenager, Carolyn and her boyfriend at that time invited me to go with them to their youth group. They demonstrated God's enthusiastic welcome. This was a time when a whole lot of mothers wouldn't let me date their daughters, but Carolyn saw the possibility of something better in me.

God does not love us because we are lovable, deserving, or have our acts together. God loves us because it is in the nature of a good parent to do so. We have no right to exclude someone God has invited to the banquet. We must welcome them in, and offer them a good seat, regardless of their past.

Jesus says to you and me, "Love as I have loved you. Show that same love to others. Not just to the people you respect—the lovable and righteous—but also to the disrespected, undesirable, and unloving of society. Jesus said that whenever we serve these "undesirables," we are really serving him. "I was hungry and you gave me food," he said. "I was thirsty and you gave me something to drink, I was a stranger and you welcomed me, I was naked and you gave me clothing, I was sick and you took care of me, I was in prison and you visited me" (Matthew 25:35-36). Jesus said that those who will inherit the kingdom are those who did those things "for the least of these."

One year during Holy Week, Carolyn and I were in Titusville, Florida, with our son's high school baseball team. It was 10:00 at night, and we were in a laundromat in a bad area of town, doing laundry for all twenty-one players. It reeked of urine and booze, and bars covered the windows. We were there at our own risk. In the corner sat a street person who appeared to not have all his wits about him. He had taken off all his clothes and was washing them in the washer, just standing there, naked.

I began to look around, and I recognized that that laundromat was just the sort of place where Jesus hangs out. These are the people with whom Jesus lives! All of a sudden, it was Holy Week, and I was recognizing the presence of Jesus. My heart began to sing the music of the risen Christ, and I began to tell some of the other baseball parents who were there about how God did incredible things by creating each one of us. We were holding church at 10:00 at night in a Titusville laundromat, and Jesus was right there with us, in us.

When you have been invaded by the presence of God, you have one purpose in the world: to be a witness of Jesus Christ. A lot of people in the church today confuse witnessing with an attitude of "God told me to tell you. . . ." Being a witness and trying to speak for God are not the same thing. There is a fine line between the two. So many times we try to tell other people the will of God in their lives, rather than that God's desire is simply to live in them, period.

Putting in Our Sweat Equity

If there is going to be a banquet like the one Jesus described, somebody has to sweat in the kitchen. Ross Dillahunt is a long-time member of Ginghamsburg who really lives out a sweat theology. He truly understands Jesus' question, "Ross, do you love me?" working diligently to connect with those who are not already at the table.

He has experienced firsthand the importance of being invited. "Fifteen years ago," he says, "John Thomas invited me to a men's dinner. Ohio Congressman Tony Hall was the speaker, and I made a recommitment to Christ after hearing his talk."

Several years after that, Ross thought the Lord wanted him to start a fellowship of some kind at the car dealership where he works. As he explains, "We started a Bible study there, and I kept inviting the guys to come, but the only ones showing up were those who were already Christians—and there weren't very many of them! So, we changed the format a little and decided to have a monthly men's breakfast in the conference room of the dealership. We bring in a Christian speaker who shares a personal story or a message. My wife, Pam, cooks the breakfast, and the salesmen eagerly show up." Now there's a couple that really knows the literal value of sweat equity—especially Pam!

God wants us to be involved—to do our part in the transformation of the world for God's kingdom. When some of us pray, we say, "O Lord, help my relationship with my spouse to be intimate and deep." Then we sit back and wonder why it doesn't happen by next week. We fail to plant the seeds God gives us, and then expect to reap what we did not sow.

Everything, from raising our children to business ventures to church planting, is about investment and partnership with God. "Whoever sows sparingly will also reap sparingly, and whoever sows generously will also reap generously" (2 Corinthians 9:6 NIV).

A farmer and his friend were standing by a field of ripe wheat, which was ready to harvest. The friend looked at the bounteous field and said, "Doesn't God do a marvelous job?" The farmer replied, "You should have seen the field when God had it by himself!"

God doesn't work alone. God is in the seed business. With our consumer mentality, we expect God to give us fully ripened fruit, but more often God's mission is a partnership of investment that depends on you and me. We are not here to be consumers; we are here to be conceivers. We are to become pregnant with God's purpose, and give birth to the work of God's kingdom.

Chances are you've barely begun to break ground in your life on what God can accomplish through the Holy Spirit. It's time to break up your unplowed ground, your unrealized potential as a leader. When you act on God's promise, the outcome will always be greater than your expectation. We need to bring more people to the table than others think possible, welcome more people than others think wise, and serve more people than others think practical. We must take action and do for God and the world what we never thought possible.

One Church That's UnLearning

Lutheran Church of Hope, West Des Moines, Iowa
www.hopewdm.org

- **Quick Description:** Reaching out to the world around us to share the everlasting love of Jesus Christ, becoming a Spirited, growing, and Christ-centered community filled with hope.
- **History:** Evangelical Lutheran Church in America (ELCA); started 1993.
- **Attendance:** Over 5,000 in six weekend services, 250-300 at the Thursday night "Immersion" service, which focuses on the generations of postmodern culture.

"Our congregation has become rather intergenerational without much effort. About nine years ago, we tried to do a 'Gen-X' service, got several hundred people to attend, and then were promptly told by those several hundred that they wanted to worship with people who were different from themselves. Our response was to do a very counterintuitive thing and mix the postmoderns with the moderns. To this day the average age at weekend worship remains in the early thirties.

"Nonetheless, we discovered there was a significant group of people under thirty in our city we were not reaching. In 2004 we launched 'Immersion,' an on-site satellite congregation where all are welcome but the focus is on people between the ages of eighteen and thirty. This ministry includes all the components of a healthy congregation: worship, discipleship, community life, and servant ministry opportunities.

"Our mission statement affirms that we are a church of individuals, different in many ways, yet called together by God to be one in ministry and mission. We like unchurched people, and we know what a difference Jesus can make in their lives. For this reason, we seek to reach out to the world around us and share the everlasting love of Christ, even through our worship."

—Richard Webb, Associate Pastor, has been with the church since 2000; age: late forties

Conclusion

Pressing Forward with Open Arms

UnLearning leaders are visionaries, experiencing the future today through their thoughts, words, and actions, and calling others to join in this God-journey. Press forward with a clear purpose to change the world for Christ, by loving and serving others as Jesus did.

The world is waiting for the reality of God's presence to be demonstrated through you. We must unLearn the notion of faith being simply the absence of doubt. Faith is acting on what God says, following God's directive at any given time, pressing forward no matter what.

Many of us wish we had more faith. But that's not really what we need. We simply need to act on the measure of faith we've already received through God's grace. We need to keep looking forward to bigger and better things, "to the city that has foundations, whose architect and builder is God" (Hebrews 11:10b). UnLearning leadership demands a forward focus. As Jesus said, "No one who puts a hand to the plow and looks back is fit for the kingdom of God" (Luke 9:62).

Remember what happened to Lot's wife? God told Lot's family to leave the intensely negative environment found in the city of Sodom, to get out or else be destroyed. God warned them that once they started moving, heading toward a better place, they must not look back and become distracted by the past. But Lot's wife looked back. She couldn't let go of the familiar habits and defeating behavior patterns that gave her comfort and security. She looked back and became permanently a part of that godforsaken place. The paralysis of fear from the dysfunction of her past became the reality of her existence.

We can become so bogged down with the trappings and trivialities of this world that we lose our focus on the mission to which God is calling us. I can't believe how often people tell me that God doesn't speak to them. Chances are, they've simply become distracted.

From Eyes Wide Shut to Arms Wide Open

Jesus kept his focus on the mission by beginning each day in relationship with his Father, learning what made God's heart cry, and taking action to heal those hurts God sees in the world. Sometimes it seems easier to just block out the pain God wants us to see. Carolyn and I were watching television after working hard one day. The program was about children with cancer. It was gut-wrenching, and not at all what we needed to unwind after a busy day. We looked at each other and said "Enough!" and turned off the show.

Isn't that easy to do? We build insulated cocoons to protect ourselves, closing our eyes to the suffering of others. We end up living in a narrow, superficial, selfish delusion of well-being.

One way I deal with stress is through humor. As a kid, I was the family comedian. When things got bad at school, I'd work especially hard at home on my comedy routines. More than once, when my clowning around the house became extreme, my dad told my mom, "You'd better call the principal because obviously he's failing something again."

I was the epitome of superficial, my masking laughter motivated by denial. This is what Jesus means when he says to people who follow him, in effect, "You have eyes to see, but you don't see. And you have ears to hear, but you're not getting it." (See Matthew 13:16-23.) He warns against the temptation to guard ourselves so well we become oblivious to others' needs and God's desires for our lives.

As a result, we do church lite. We enjoy awesome music, sing songs from the heart, study the Bible with passion, and tell our stories. We feel inspired, but we go out oblivious to lost and hurting people all around us. As the prophet observed in Isaiah 58, we go through all the right religious motions, feeling good about ourselves and our spirituality, but God is not laughing.

We might change the channel, but God doesn't. As James 5:1-6 and other passages teach, God hears the cries of people we don't hear. God hears the cries of the people we've hurt, oppressed, and cut out of the abundance we experience. God seeks that which is lost and restores that which is broken. "Lament and mourn and weep. Let your laughter be turned into mourning and your joy into dejection" (James 4:9). We are to align our hearts with God's heart. We are to cry about the things God cries about.

UnLearning leaders must personally grieve with God. Ask yourself: "Does my heart ache for God's purposes to be fulfilled in every life, in every corner of the world?" "Does this attitude permeate my leadership in Christ's church?" "Am I helping those in my congregation build cocoons to insulate themselves from a suffering world, or am I helping them reach out?"

Several years back, when the Ethiopian food crisis was at its peak, I was struck by the images of horrifying poverty and malnutrition that covered the news stations each night. I was tempted to change the channel, to live in my protected bubble.

Instead, we figured out a way to act on it as a church. We led a multiple-week challenge to sponsor children through World Vision. The response was powerful. The people of Ginghamsburg adopted more than 260 children. To this day my wife and I still sponsor a needy overseas child.

Paying the Price

Giving money is always good, but we also must lead our people to do more than give money. More important is their personal investment of time and energy. In a typical year, dozens of teams go out from Ginghamsburg on mission, financing it out of their own resources. Thirty teams have traveled to the Gulf Coast region to help in the rebuilding process in the aftermath of Hurricane Katrina. Our New Path ministry helps find housing for single moms here in our community. Jim Taylor, who runs a Ford dealership nearby, sponsors hot lunches for the homeless. Louella Thompson, supported financially and assisted by many Ginghamsburg small groups, feeds the hungry daily in nearby Middletown, Ohio.

Some four hundred teenagers give one or more afternoons a week to reach out to kids in the inner city of Dayton and throughout the Miami valley, working with at-risk kids in remedial math, reading, faith-based teachings, sports, and arts. Over the years, Clubhouse has empowered more than nine hundred teens to go out and do local ministry. They have started Clubhouses in Cincinnati, and at Miami University in Oxford, Ohio. There are also five teen-initiated Clubhouses in South Carolina, and some as far away as the Czech Republic. Clubhouse is more than tutoring and racial reconciliation. The mission of Clubhouse is to train and equip teens to go out and be the hands and feet of Jesus in neighborhoods where a lot of adults probably wouldn't go. According to Cheryl Bender, longtime director of Clubhouse, "These neighborhood kids are discipled. What happens is like our adult discipleship groups or our home groups. These kids become attached to our teens. Many have come to a faith relationship with Jesus Christ."

Jesus taught that the good shepherd will "leave the ninety-nine in the wilderness and go after the one that is lost until he finds it" (Luke 15:4b). The good shepherd gets up and goes out after the one in need. What are you willing to risk in order to go after those who are lost? What is the price you are willing to pay?

You'll keep the godfathers and godmothers of your church very happy if you continue doing church the way you've always done it—without any risk or change. But we don't have time to play the kingdom of church. We have time only to obey one voice— the voice of God. Do *not* settle for anything less than God's creative purpose.

UnLearning means going in new directions. It requires following fresh winds of the Holy Spirit. UnLearning leads you to new places where God is moving. When leaders and congregations let go of what they thought they knew about doing church, they will be led by the Spirit into simply *being* the church, living for God in everything they do. Faithful communities will emerge that are effectively reaching unchurched populations for Jesus Christ in a postmodern, post-Christian world. Each local expression of this vision is distinct, yet the smell of the same God hovers over them all.

In the business world, when you achieve success, you often become important, visible, or famous. We tend to mimic that in the church—judging our success by whether we have a better place at the table, more fame, and more fortune than we did last year.

UnLearning leaders are willing to forsake that kind of success and accomplishment to live in the shadows so that God can work through them. Like Moses, we may not achieve the place of promise in our lifetime, but that's not the point. What matters is that God lives large through our lives.

Radical church is hard. In my years of following Jesus, I've never known one year to go by without painful struggles. I would prefer a life of ease, but Jesus didn't call us to be comfortable.

Most churches are full of parents and grandparents who would willingly give their lives to save their children, but some of us aren't even willing to give up certain music styles or worship practices to reach the next generation. It is not the big things that will stop the kingdom of God, but the little ones.

To get bigger, sometimes we might have to get smaller. Many of Jesus' disciples walked away when they encountered the high cost of discipleship, but some were willing to pay the price, knowing that living out God's kingdom was worth the personal cost.

You can empower a group of people committed to radically demonstrating the love of Jesus Christ in your world.

Start by unLearning.

God is doing a new thing with an emerging generation of leaders and churches.

Be there.

Notes

1. Born to Be Wild

1. Michael G. Maudlin, "God's Contractor," *Christianity Today* (14 June, 1999), www.christianitytoday.com/ct/9t7/9t7044.html.

2. C. Kirk Hadaway, Penny Long Marier, and Mark Chaves, "What the Polls Don't Show: A Closer Look at U.S. Church Attendance," *American Sociological Review*, vol. 58, no. 6 (6 December, 1993), 741-52.

3. Reginald W. Bibby, *There's Got to Be More: Connecting Churches and Canadians* (Winfield, BC: Wood Lake Books, 1995), 16.

2. From Broadcast to Narrowcast

1. Faith Popcorn and Lys Marigold, *Clicking* (New York: HarperCollins, 1996), 145.

2. Michael Slaughter with Warren Bird, *Real Followers* (Nashville: Abingdon, 1999), 15-16.

4. Thriving in Paradox

1. *Emerging Trends for Effective Ministry in the 21st Century Church*, American Society for Church Growth, (November, 2000), side one.

2. Various collections of worship videos produced by Ginghamsburg are available through our e-store at http://www.ginghamsburgglobal.org/Merchant2/merchant.mvc.

3. Mike Slaughter and Kim Miller, "Next Level Churches—A Multisensory Experience," *Rev!* (September–October, 2000), 84.

4. Patricia Davis, "How Technology Has Changed the Way We Attend Church," *Wall Street Journal* (13 November, 2000), R28-R29.

5. Michael Paulson, "On Ash Wednesday, a Wider Observance," *Boston Globe* (28 February, 2001).

7. Replicating the DNA

1. *Dictionary of Daily Life of Indians of the Americas*, vol. 2 (Newport Beach, Calif.: American Indian Publishers, 1981), 739.

8. Moving Together

1. Peter F. Drucker, *The Essential Drucker* (New York: HarperCollins, 2001).

9. A Higher Value

1. Wayne Cordiero, *Doing Church as a Team* (Ventura, Calif.: Regal, 2001), 25.

2. Skip Hollandsworth, "The Real Troy Aikman," *Texas Monthly* (December, 1998).

10. A Theology of Sweat

1. *The Master Christian Library, vols. 1-4, Sage Digital Library*, "John Wesley" (Sage Software, 1995).

2. F. F. Bruce, *Commentary on the Book of Acts* (Grand Rapids: Eerdmans, 1977), 241.

3. Robert Smith, *Augsburg Commentary on the New Testament: Matthew* (Minneapolis: Augsburg, 1989), 103.

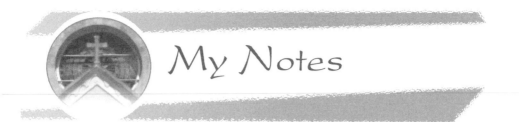

My Notes

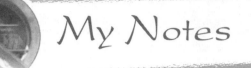

My Notes

Principles for discovering a life of faith, balance, and purpose in all aspiring leaders

newly revised and updated!

- Outlines five crucial disciplines for anyone wanting to hone leadership skills:
    - **D**evotion to God
    - **R**eadiness for lifelong learning
    - **I**nvesting in key relationships
    - **V**isioning for the future
    - **E**ating and exercise for life

ISBN 978-0-687-65009-5

- Leadership inspiration drawn from Scripture, pop culture, and Slaughter's own ministry

- Each chapter includes devotional questions for reflection

- Church-wide program resources available separately

Published by

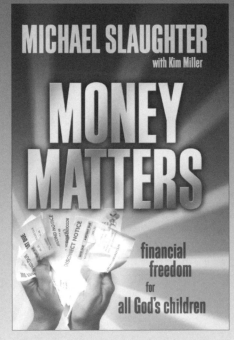

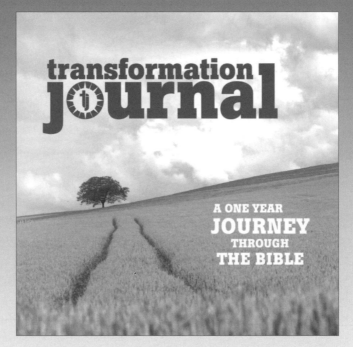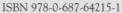